THE

BOOK OF

GAME-BREAKER
BASEBALL

THE

125
Louisville Slugger®
Louisville, Kentucky Made In U.S.A.

BOOK OF

GAME-BREAKER
BASEBALL

How to Master 30 of the Game's
Most Difficult Plays

John Monteleone
and Mark Gola

A Mountain Lion Book

Contemporary Books

Chicago   New York   San Francisco   Lisbon   London   Madrid   Mexico City
Milan   New Delhi   San Juan   Seoul   Singapore   Sydney   Toronto

Library of Congress Cataloging-in-Publication Data

Monteleone, John J.
    The Louisville Slugger book of game-breaker baseball : how to master 30 of the
game's most difficult plays / by John J. Monteleone & Mark Gola.
        p.   cm.
    "A Mountain Lion book."
    ISBN 0-07-138561-4
    1. Baseball.   I. Gola, Mark.   II. Title.

GV867.M56   2002
796.357—dc21   2002020779

Contemporary Books

A Division of The McGraw·Hill Companies

1 2 3 4 5 6 7 8 9 0   VLP/VLP   1 0 9 8 7 6 5 4 3 2

ISBN 0-07-138561-4

This book was set in Sabon by Ellen Kollmon
Printed and bound by Vicks Lithograph

Cover and interior design by Nick Panos
Cover photos, clockwise from top left: Derek Jeter © Tom Hauck/Allsport, Mike Hampton © Jeff
Gross/Allsport, Sean Casey © Mark Lyons/Allsport, Alex Rodriguez © Ronald Martinez/Allsport
Interior photographs by Mike Plunkett

McGraw-Hill books are available at special quantity discounts to use as premiums and sales
promotions, or for use in corporate training programs. For more information, please write to the
Director of Special Sales, Professional Publishing, McGraw-Hill, Two Penn Plaza, New York, NY
10121-2298. Or contact your local bookstore.

This book is printed on acid-free paper.

To Bill Leary of the Lambertville (NJ) Indians, who first showed me how to "take two and hit to right," a solid-gold game-breaker tactic (#7) in the book for the ages.

—J.J.M.

To two great coaches, Stan Davis and Sonny Pittaro. Thank you for your teachings, guidance, and, finally, friendship. The baseball field acted as your forum, but the lessons gathered from your "coaching" extend far beyond the white lines.

—M.G.

CONTENTS

SECTION III PITCHING

SECTION IV BASERUNNING

ACKNOWLEDGMENTS

First, thanks to Rob Taylor, editor at Contemporary Books, for his continued support and friendship.

Thanks to Bill Williams, vice president of Advertising and Marketing at Hillerich and Bradsby, for his trust in representing Louisville Slugger®.

Thank you to Mike Plunkett, photographer, for his exceptional work behind the camera. Mike's professional expertise is what allows our instructional text to come to life.

Thanks to the baseball players at Rider University who volunteered their time to participate in the photo shoot: Rich Brooks, Jared Carle, Casey Long, Bryan Merrigan, Erinn Pesaresi, and Kevin Riley. Best of luck to the Broncs in the 2002 season.

Thanks to Rick Freeman, baseball aficionado, for cracking open his treasure chest of archival gems that provided several bites of baseball history for anecdotal reference.

A special thanks to Sonny Pittaro, head baseball coach at Rider University, for unlocking the gates to his sacred grounds at Richard F. Daly Field.

Thanks to Joan Mohan at Mountain Lion, Inc.

INTRODUCTION

This book is for the player who wants to excel at the game of baseball. And it is for the player who wants to prepare himself to move up to higher levels of competition. It is for any youth league player trying to make a starting lineup or scholastic player aspiring to make the varsity team. *The Louisville Slugger® Book of Game-Breaker Baseball* explains and demonstrates how to master the advanced skills of baseball, the skills that can make a difference in winning a game. The following pages of *Game-Breaker Baseball* include 30 of these most difficult plays and skills.

Game-Breaker Baseball supplements and builds on the instruction of those books that explain the basics. For example, where a basic book on hitting would explain the rudiments of hitting, *Game-Breaker Baseball*'s treatment explains how a right-handed batter can hit a ball to the opposite field, or how a left-handed batter can hook a ball to the pull side of the field. These are "game-breaker" skills because they're precision skills applied in certain recognizable situations that help move runners into scoring position or score them, and thus break open games. They're the skills and plays that not only win games but also draw the comment that all players covet hearing, "He knows how to play the game."

The treatment is divided into separate sections on hitting, fielding, pitching, and baserunning. Readers should read and study each entry separately, apply and practice the instruction, and then return to reread the instruction. Doing so will enable you not only to master the desired skill but also to appreciate the many nuances of the particular skill or play.

Players should pay special attention to the situations in which these advanced skills are best applied. Some are self-evident, such as two-strike and zone hitting when at bat, but others—such as hitting the curveball, or hook sliding, or throwing a change-up—call for total concentration and instant awareness of when and how to act.

The skills presented in this distinct treatment should be undertaken at the proper age. Advanced pitching techniques, such as throwing a curveball, should not be attempted until the body is strong enough to endure the torque and stress brought on by the pitching motion, particularly the external shoulder rotation of the throwing-side arm. However, a pitcher's technique when covering first base or learning how to slide can be safely (and productively) undertaken at any age.

The time it takes to master the 30 skills and plays of *Game-Breaker Baseball* will vary significantly. Some may take as much as a year or two, or sometimes longer. For example, hitting the curveball or expanding the strike zone can take several years to master, while the push bunt or pop-up slide can be mastered in a relatively short time. But the important thing is to learn the proper technique and then practice it over and over. If you stick with it, you'll eventually master it, and you'll soon be making a pivotal play on a regular basis in games of your own.

THE

BOOK OF

GAME-BREAKER
BASEBALL

HITTING

Introduction

It's been said time and time again how difficult it is to hit a round ball with a round bat. It's difficult, but not impossible. By taking swing after swing and hitting ball after ball, you develop a sixth sense that helps you find the ball with the barrel with increasing consistency. Soon, your personal hitting zone evolves. Pitches are thrown in certain areas of the strike zone and you pulverize the ball with subconscious effort. Conversely, there are other areas of the strike zone that you survey with distaste.

Gradually, the type of hitter you are becomes more defined. Some hitters are "dead fastball hitters," who await the hard stuff, sit back, and explode on incoming pitches. Other hitters are more rhythmic, sometimes guessing at pitches early in the count before becoming more conservative as the count deepens. They are better hitters with two strikes.

Even the types of hits you produce become predictable. There are flyball hitters, line-drive hitters, and contact hitters who produce mostly ground balls. Furthermore, hitters are classified by where they hit the ball and are known as pull hitters, opposite-field hitters, or a select few who learn to use the entire field of play called spray hitters.

These elements define the type of hitter you are and how you perform. And at advanced levels of play, pitchers use this profile data to get you out. That's part of what makes them your enemy. Observant pitchers, catchers, and coaches recognize a hitter's tendencies and combat them by avoiding strengths and exploiting weaknesses. If you like the hard stuff, they'll serve up soft stuff. When they see that you punish pitches up in the strike zone, they'll throw pitches at the knees or below. If you love to pull the ball, the only strikes you'll sniff are those thrown to the outside part of the plate. And even if you do get a pitch you like and can pull, the fielders will be positioned in areas that defend your individual patterns. Hitting is difficult not simply because the ball is round and the bat is round. The pitcher, the catcher, and seven other men in the field play a fairly significant role as well.

A Well-Rounded Offensive Asset

As you progress in levels of baseball, your ability to execute and produce in a variety of situations must expand for you to remain an offensive threat. Whether you like to hear it or not, you're going to have to learn to hit a curveball. If you don't, you're an easy out in the lineup. It's time to grow up and confront your weaknesses. As longtime Rider University head coach Sonny Pittaro would utter to his freshman hitters who struggled to adjust to college pitching, "Call your mom and dad and tell them the pitchers are throwing you curveballs."

Becoming a well-rounded hitter entails more than hitting different types of pitches thrown to varying locations. You have to be capable of performing duties that help your team win ballgames. Everyone must learn to bunt. Bunting is a skill that may seldom be used, but is extremely critical in big-game situations. If it's in the late innings, and your team is down by one run, you'd better be able to lay down a sacrifice bunt to advance your teammate into scoring position. Bunting is a simple skill that is often neglected in practice. It requires proper technique and light maintenance. That's it. There is no excuse for being a poor bunter.

Other offensive skills include drag bunting, slashing, hitting ground balls to the right side of second base, and lifting balls in the air for a sacrifice fly. The ability to execute these offensive plays is crucial. They can make a significant impact on the outcome of a game. Your goal is to be a great hitter, and also to execute efficiently in situations that necessitate specific results. Base hits up the middle and doubles down the third-base line are not always required for you to contribute to your team's offense.

By mastering these advanced hitting techniques, you'll improve as a hitter and increase your value to the ball club. Learn how to execute the fundamentals of these skills during individual batting sessions. From there, sharpen your skills in daily batting practice by dedicating a few minutes to situational swings.

HITTING THE CURVEBALL

"A good hitter will always look for the fastball [because] he can adjust his timing for the slower curve and change of pace. But if he is looking for the curve, the fastball will be thrown by him."
—LEFTY O'DOUL

Hitting would be a lot easier if pitchers just threw fastballs, but the curveball has been complicating the game since shortly after the Civil War. As baseball lore has it, a man named William Arthur "Candy" Cummings is credited with the introduction of the curveball.

Identifying the Curveball

The first thing we need to know and understand is the precise nature of a curveball and how it differs from a fastball. While the fastball is predominantly straight, the curveball goes down and to one side or the other, depending on the pitcher. The velocity of the curveball is slower than a fastball's.

The curveball appears to leave the pitcher's hand with a slight upward and outward arc. The fastball leaves the pitcher's hand at a slightly downward angle with the pitcher's palm facing the batter. The rotation on the curveball is a forward and slightly sideward spin. When you see the pitcher's palm facing toward his throwing-side ear, look for a breaking pitch. The first indication is a slight arc that the ball travels just as it is released.

The fastball appears to explode out of the pitcher's hand, while there is a slight delay when the curveball is released. The speed of the curveball is slower. Major league curveballs travel 12 to 15 mph slower than fastballs. When a pitcher throws a curveball at a significantly reduced speed it throws the batter off balance and upsets his timing. Change-ups have a similar effect, although change-of-pace pitches usually travel slower than breaking balls.

Hitting the Deuce

So now that you know what a curveball looks like and how it behaves, how do you hit it?

Early recognition is critical. The sooner you identify the curveball the easier it is to make the adjustments. Concentrate on quickly identifying the pitch as it is released from the pitcher's hand. As soon as you've recognized the curveball, follow these steps to hit it.

The hitter is fooled by a breaking pitch. Once the hands commit to the ball, the batter has very little chance of hitting the ball with authority. Because the front knee bends, the rear leg collapses and the hips are unable to rotate. All power from the lower body is lost.

1. Stride softly, as if stepping on thin ice, a very short distance, perhaps four to six inches. Keep the toe closed. If you use a front leg kick when you stride, make sure that you do not prematurely drop your front foot. The keys here are to separate the front leg and hands from the core of the body yet keep the hips from uncoiling too soon. Engage the swing but keep the hands back and the torso, or top of the body, over the legs. Do not transfer your weight entirely onto or over the front leg, which leaves no foundation for uncoiling or rotating.

2. As you engage and continue the swing—with the left arm and left side leading—keep the barrel of the bat trailing behind the hands.

3. Swing where the pitch will be, not where you see it. Calculate the pitch's break and adjust your swing. (Recognizing what type of breaking ball and how much it breaks is information you should gather while waiting on deck and watching the pitcher warm up.) If the pitch appears to be thigh-high, it will probably cross the plate around your knees. Adjust to the break or you'll swing over the pitch.

It's important to keep the hands back when a curveball is thrown. When you're behind in the count, look to hit the ball to the opposite field by minimizing hip rotation and letting the ball travel deeper into the hitting zone.

4. Shorten your swing. The shorter the swing the longer you can wait to commit your hands. Long swings must be initiated as the pitch is released. You have to decide the location of your swing as soon as you see the ball. Shorten your swing and you'll increase the time you have to see the pitch.

5. Look to hit the ball to the opposite field. Because of the decreased velocity, hitters often try to pull breaking pitches, thereby making contact too far out in front of the plate and producing weak ground balls to the pull side or infield pop-ups. Telling yourself to hit the ball to the opposite field will keep you on the ball longer, lock your front shoulder in, and allow you to hit breaking pitches with authority.

6. Imagine a hitting area—a large horizontal oval—just above and to the opposite field-side of the pitcher's head and picture hitting a line drive right into that target area, which will keep you from over-rotating and promote a flat but slightly ascending swing plane.

7. Hold the hands in a right-hand palm up, left-hand palm down position (for right-handed batters) until the knob of the bat passes by the belly button and reaches the heel of the front foot. Make bat/ball contact with the palm up, palm down hand position. After the ball leaves the bat roll the right hand over and finish with a full extension of both arms.

Your belly button, or midpoint of the torso, points toward center field or right-center field upon completion of the follow-through. Brace your weight on the entire front foot but do not fully rotate the toe open as required when "turning on a pitch," that is, when fully rotating on a pitch located over the middle or inside part of the plate.

Keep your lower body "quieter," that is, do not rotate explosively. Maintain a vigorous athletic movement, but not so fast that you upset your timing and thus bring your backside and top hand into the hitting area so quickly that you pull or hook the ball.

One strategic note: If it's early in an at-bat, or you're ahead in the count, don't swing at any breaking balls (unless they're hangers). You'll find that pitchers frequently miss the strike zone with curveballs, because it's not just a hard pitch to hit, it's a hard pitch to consistently throw for strikes. Besides, why swing at a pitch you struggle with unless you have to?

On breaking balls thrown below the belt (left), keep your hands back and quiet your hips. Don't try to do too much with the pitch. Hanging curveballs (right), however, should be attacked and driven for power. Notice how the hips have fired, that is, fully opened, allowing the barrel to make contact out in front of home plate.

DRILL

You can practice hitting curveballs very effectively by using Wiffle balls. Have someone pitch from about 25 feet. To make a Wiffle ball curve, place your index and middle finger along the equator that divides the solid hemisphere and the perforated hemisphere, thumb underneath. Deliver the throw from an overhand or three-quarter-release point. It will break down and away. Take 50 swings in five sets of 10. Your goal is to hit 9 of every 10 curveballs correctly—solid line drives to the opposite field or back through the pitcher's box.

HITTING BREAKING BALLS

Major league third baseman Scott Rolen believes that:

"The most important element to hitting a breaking ball is letting it get to you. It's much easier said than done. You hear people all the time saying, "Stay back, stay back," but it's difficult to do if you're looking at a fastball. The bottom line is it's not that easy to hit a breaking ball. You can put yourself in a position to hit a breaking ball as best you can, and I do that by looking for a fastball on the outer half of the plate. If I look for a fastball in, I'm going to be too quick to open up and won't be able to wait long enough for an off-speed pitch. I look for a pitch away because you naturally have to wait longer on a pitch away.

"The other key is that I try to make the breaking ball be up to hit it. Breaking balls down and away, you're not supposed to hit those pitches. Those are pitcher's pitches. The idea is not to swing at them. Attack the breaking balls that are up, ones that are hanging a little bit, ones that are more middle-in. The ones down and away you should leave. If you have two strikes, you have to try to do something. Maybe spoil the pitch by fouling it off, but unless you have two strikes on you leave that pitch alone."

2

HITTING THE CHANGE-UP

If you want to learn how to hit a change-of-pace or change-up, first take heed of what's taught to pitchers about the benefits of this pitch. Hall of Fame pitcher Warren Spahn said, "Hitting is timing. Pitching is upsetting timing." What better way to upset the hitter's timing than delivering a pitch that arrives later than expected! Throw off a batter's timing and you take away his power.

Another Hall of Fame member, Stan Musial, a lifetime .331 hitter who faced Warren Spahn's change-up many times, reveals how he combated its effectiveness: "I learned I had to give in, to go to the opposite field against him, to wait on the ball a split second longer, or I wouldn't have had a chance."

According to Larry Anderson, former major league relief pitcher, "You don't just want the hitters moving in and out, but forward and back." Again, it's the change-up that the pitcher employs to get batters leaning too far forward, which prevents them from hitting the ball with any authority.

Uncovering the Change-Up

What is a change-up and how do you recognize it? A change-up is simply a pitch that looks like a fastball but travels at a reduced speed. Some change-ups have a sinking movement or tailing action, but all travel at a significantly reduced speed. Good change-ups are well disguised. Pitchers throw them without changing their deliveries in any way. As a batter, you see the same leg lift, same stride, and same arm speed. If a pitcher alters any of these elements, you may be able to detect it before the ball is released.

A change-up is extremely effective because it is so difficult to identify. It looks like a fastball as it's released out of the pitcher's hand.

Use the Opposite Field

Because the change-up is thrown with many different kinds of grips, its spin and arc are not consistently the same. The spin is often backward, like that of a fastball, but slower. With certain grips pitchers can impart some sidespin as well, which makes the ball move down and sideways.

How do you adjust to hit the change-up? Stan Musial's approach—that is, to take the pitch to the opposite field, is a good start. And keep in mind the techniques we recommend for hitting the curveball. There are a lot of similarities in the approaches. Shortening your swing and looking to hit the ball to the opposite field will help you to successfully hit the change-up.

When you take the ball to the opposite field you are able to keep the bat level longer. Keep the hands in a bottom-hand palm down, top-hand palm up position through the hitting zone. This position gives you the opportunity to lift a line drive over the infield or drive a hard ground ball through an infield hole. Hooking or pulling a change-up requires more

The key to hitting the change-up is to keep your hands back and stay behind the ball. If you're able to do that, a change-up simply becomes a slow fastball

Because hitters perceive the change-up to be a fastball, their hips and hands fire prematurely. Their weight shifts out over their front leg, and they're forced to slow their swing speed to make contact with the pitch. The final result: a weakly hit ball.

perfect timing because the bat moves more quickly off the swing plane when you roll the head of the bat with the top hand. If a pitcher puts a change-up in a poor location, that is, he throws it up or inside in the strike zone, you will be able to hit it with some pop. And many of them you'll be able to pull successfully.

However, if you try to pull change-ups that are down and away in the strike zone, you'll hit weak ground balls. Rather, keep your hands back and take the pitches to the opposite field.

Pitchers who have not properly mastered the change-up often tip the pitch. Here are some things to look for:

- A delivery motion that is faster than normal
- Arm or body motion that is suddenly slowed or decelerated
- Pushing of the throwing hand deep into the pocket when gripping the ball
- More than two fingers wrapped around the ball

The best way to approach hitting a change-up is to think about hitting the ball to the opposite-field gap. When you hit to the opposite fielder, rotate your hips no further than a point at which your belly button faces the pitcher.

DRILL

All pitches other than the fastball have the potential to throw off a batter's timing. So this drill will be universally useful and applicable to learning how to handle any off-speed pitch.

1. Use a bungee cord, hospital rubber band, thin strip of bicycle tube, or some other elastic band, approximately five feet long. Assume a normal batting stance and wrap the band around your lead arm at the biceps and grip the end of the band in your top hand while gripping the bat.

2. Have a pitcher throw three sets of 10 pitches, alternating fastballs and change-ups. Stride but don't swing. Concentrate on keeping the same amount of tension in the rubber band for all pitches. Also try to keep the upper body from moving too far forward over the front leg. The rubber band will help by pulling the front side closed as you separate the hands and bat from the rear of the body. Remember, by keeping the hands back and not letting them drift too far forward you will be able to deliver the bat head at the latest possible moment.

3. Repeat three sets of 10 pitches without the pitcher announcing the type of pitch. Concentrate on making the same controlled movement on each pitch. Check to see that you have not allowed the upper body to drift too far forward. If your front leg has bowed significantly—the result of receiving and then stabilizing an excessive weight shift—you've gone too far forward with your upper body.

4. Repeat one set of 10 pitches without announcing the type of pitch. Make a full swing, driving the balls where they're pitched. This sequence includes hitting some of the very vulnerable change-up mistakes (up or inside in the strike zone) to the pull side and change-ups down and away to the opposite field.

3

HOOKING A BALL

"One of the most common—but bedeviling—situations in the game. The object seems simple: Hit the ball on the ground to the right side, moving the runner into scoring position. It becomes more important when moving a runner from second to third, where he can score on a wild pitch, error, groundout, sacrifice fly, or base hit."

—ROD CAREW

Hooking a ball is an advanced form of situational hitting. Although hooking can be done by batters from either side of the plate, it is usually employed by a left-handed batter who wants to pull the ball to the right side of the field to advance a runner from second base to third base or to score a runner from third base.

The mechanics of hooking a ball require the batter to meet the ball in front of the plate with the barrel of the bat well ahead of the hands (closer to the fair side of home plate).

Acknowledging the Game Situation

When you reach the higher levels of baseball, you need more than just good basic hitting skills. You need awareness. Every time you go up to bat you need to know the score, what inning it is, how many outs there are, who—if anyone—is on base, what their capabilities are, who's on deck, and if there's any sign on. You're part of a team, and your strategy at the plate should reflect that.

At every level of baseball it's the little things that often win games. With the exception of a home run, every hit or walk needs another hit, walk, ground ball, or fly ball to score a run, so a hitter who is always aware of the offensive situation can be irreplaceable to a team.

When coming to the plate, size up the situation. If you bat left-handed, consider hooking a ball when a teammate has gotten on base ahead of you. Here are the key situations in which a left-handed batter would try to hook a ball.

1. Leadoff batter reaches first base, leaving a wide hitting lane between the second baseman and the first baseman, who has to hold the runner close to the bag.

2. Leadoff batter reaches second base, thus setting up a situation in which he can score without another base hit. Your objective would be to hit a ground ball to the right side of the infield, a fly ball to right or right-center field, or a base hit to the right side of the field.

3. Man on third with less than two outs. You may have a bases-loaded situation, men on second and third base, or men on first and third base. Your objective is to score the runner from third with a ground ball to the right side, a ground ball through the infield, or a fly ball or base hit to the outfield.

For a left-handed batter, the top hand needs to become more active when attempting to hook a ball to the right side of second base. The bat should be angled to the pull side at the point of contact.

Get the bat started early and rotate your hips when attempting to hit the ball to the right side. Hitting the ball out in front of home plate produces favorable results in this situation.

Pitches on the inner half of the plate are much easier to pull. If your job is to advance the runner from second base, jump on an inside strike.

How do you hook the ball? First, move slightly closer to the plate. This will allow you to reach more pitches on the outer edge of the strike zone. Look for pitches inside and off-speed, which will be easier to pull or hook to the right side of the diamond. Get the swing—and thus the head or barrel of the bat—started early. Allow the top hand to take over the swing earlier, that is, let it roll the head or barrel of the bat ahead of the hands just prior to impact (in a normal swing, you would refrain from rolling the top hand until after impact). This roll creates an angle at impact that directs the ball toward the batter's pull side of the field.

DRILL

Play a game of pepper with at least three other teammates, one stationed directly in front of you and flanked on each side by the others. When at bat, practice directing every other pitched ball to the player on your extreme left regardless of where the pitch is located. Be careful, even this slight flick of the wrist can dramatically increase the speed of the batted ball.

4

ZONE HITTING WITH FAVORABLE COUNTS

"I've had pitchers tell me that they used to be scared to death whenever they faced Ted Williams because they figured he always knew what was coming. Well, Ted Williams made a habit of analyzing the pitcher. He'd look for a certain pitch or for the ball to be in a certain location, depending upon the situation. If a home run can win the game, you look for a pitch you can hit for a homer. You don't swing at the first slider away . . . you wait. And if you've analyzed the pitcher you have at least some idea of when that home run ball will appear."

—CHARLEY LAU

The late Charley Lau, one of major league baseball's most accomplished batting instructors, knew full well the advanced art of hitting. As an 11-year major league catcher, he schemed with the pitcher to get batters out. However, as a batting instructor, Lau advised his students, "When you're up there at the plate facing that other guy on the mound, you're in combat. He's going to use all of his wits and all of his skill to send you back to the bench as quickly as possible. And if you don't do the same—or you don't both outthink him and outplay him—you're going to lose."

Learn the Strike Zone First

One important way to outthink and outplay the pitcher is to learn how to zone hit with favorable counts. What are we talking about here?

Hitting balls off of a tee helps you determine the areas of the strike zone where you prefer pitches, and the areas that you do not prefer.

Zone hitting is simply looking for and attacking certain pitches in specific areas of the strike zone. First, let's divide the strike zone into its basic areas. There are three horizontal areas, 1) inside or in, 2) outside or away, and 3) middle or heart of the plate; and three vertical areas, 1) low, 2) high, and 3) middle, sometimes called "right down Broadway" or "heart of the plate."

The width of the plate measures 17 inches. Its perimeter is made up of one inch of black trim. Many major league pitchers try "to paint the black," or get strikes on the very outermost parts of the plate. Tom Glavine, Greg Maddux, and Mike Mussina are three major league pitchers who are exceptional at painting the black, both up and down in the strike zone. They're known for moving the ball up, down, in, and out within (and sometimes just beyond) the strike zone.

Pitchers avoid the center of the strike zone because it's easier there for the batter to get the sweet spot of the bat on the ball. By pitching in or away the batter more often strikes the ball on the thinner handle, often

Notice the hitter was forced to pull his hands in to hit this pitch—not the type of swing you want when zone hitting. He was not looking for a pitch inside, and as a result, had to compensate his swing. When ahead in the count, make sure the pitch is in a favorable location before swinging.

getting "sawed off" (bat is broken), or on the end of the bat beyond the sweet spot.

Working the Count to Your Favor

As a hitter you can increase your chances of getting a pitch in a more hittable location or zone by working the count to your favor. Hitter's counts are 2–0 (two balls and no strikes), 3–1, and 3–0. After one or more trips to the plate against the same pitcher, 0–0, 1–0, and 2–1 can be hitter's counts, but only if you've been paying attention and logging the pattern of pitches thrown to you and to your teammates.

What kind of information do you need to zone hit successfully? You need a lot, and you need to keep it up to date constantly. You need to know the types of pitches your opponent throws, and you need to know which pitches he throws more often for strikes. You need to know his tendencies, that is, when he is likely to throw each pitch. Does he start batters with fastballs more often than breaking balls? Does he rely only on his fastball when he falls behind in the count? Will he walk a batter rather than "give in," that is, throw a pitch just out of the strike zone rather than a hittable strike when behind in the count? Does he throw a different mix of pitches when men are on base (such as more fastballs than curveballs)? When you've got "a book" on the pitcher, you're ready to zone hit.

It Pays to Study

Here is an example of zone hitting, a good one to master at the start. The count is 2–0 and you have observed throughout the game that the pitcher has thrown a fastball every time he's fallen behind in the count. It's a tie game in the later innings and your team needs to put a man in scoring position (at second base). You're leading off the inning. An extra base hit would set up a good scoring situation. You are a good low-ball hitter, and a good fastball hitter. Set up with the idea that you will look for a fastball that is over the middle of the plate or slightly inside. Gear your swing

Patience is extremely important to getting a pitch that is good to hit.

to get the barrel out in front and to drive the ball down the line or into the center field gap. If you get this pitch in the zone, attack it. If the pitcher throws a fastball away, high, or anywhere other than in the zone you're anticipating, or another pitch, such as a curveball, simply take the pitch. At worst the count is 2–1 and you've got two more strikes to use.

One final word: Learn your "personal hitting zone," that is, where above all other locations in the strike zone you prefer pitches. It could be down and in, as often is the case with left-handed batters. Or it could be middle and up, as is the case with Mets slugger Mike Piazza.

DRILL

Using a Wiffle ball, simulate pitch counts and zone hitting. Concentrate on fastballs middle and in, then fastballs away. Switch to curveballs away (taking a shot at right field). After you swing confirm the pitch location with the pitcher. Your goal is to always attack the ball in the zone you're concentrating on and to lay off pitches thrown outside the zone. Zone hitting is "opportunity come a-knocking," so don't let it pass you by.

5

TWO-STRIKE CONTACT HITTING

Two-strike hitting is hitting with the ball and strike count in favor of the pitcher, or what's commonly referred to as "pitcher's counts." These counts include 0–2 (no balls, two strikes), 1–2, and 2–2. The 2–2 count, though balls and strikes are the same, is a pitcher's count because he can still throw another ball without penalty—that is, without the batter reaching base with a walk. Thus, a pitcher often throws the 2–2 pitch to a difficult location, such as a breaking ball that attempts to "paint the black" on the outside corner.

Many believe that the 3–2 count is a hitter's count because the pitcher must either throw a strike or allow the batter to take first base with a base on balls. Others consider the 3–2 count a neutral count because neither pitcher nor batter has a marked advantage—the pitcher does not want to throw "ball four" and the batter does not want to take "strike three."

Being Worked by the Pitcher

Two-strike counts call for keen observation and knowledge of the pitcher's tendencies. However, when the pitcher can afford to throw a ball and not walk a batter, his options are increased. For example, a pitcher who has an A+ fastball but a C− breaking ball might use a favorable count to "show" or "display" the curveball, that is, throw it simply to set up the next pitch, the one with which he intends to retire you. He floats the curveball down and away, perhaps bouncing in the dirt, to upset your timing. Your mind and body are geared to his 89-mph fastball and you're shown a 76-mph breaking ball. Now, when he throws the next fastball it will seem a little faster, and tougher to catch up to.

Or, as is more likely with a power pitcher, the next delivery in a 0–2 or 1–2 count might sail up and inside just under your hands, which then gives the pitcher some extra room on the outside part of the plate. The inside pitch will get you thinking maybe he's coming back inside when he's only trying to set up the "out" pitch away. So you can see that the so-called pitcher's counts can be more difficult to hit. But they are not impossible, and here's how to approach them.

1. Slightly widen your stance, perhaps no more than an inch or two to eliminate a little of your lateral movement and enable you to pick up the pitch more quickly.

2. Choke the bat a half-inch or more to give you better bat control and help you to deliver the bat head faster.

3. Shorten your swing. Make it short and quick to the ball.

The batter sets up in his customary stance (left). Behind in the count with two strikes, however, he spreads his stance wider, flexes a little more at the knees, and chokes up on the bat, which lowers his center of gravity, improves his bat control, and gives him a better chance of making solid contact.

4. Hit the ball where it is pitched, or located. Let the pitcher's pitch location dictate where you will drive the ball. Think, "I will take what the pitcher gives me and drive the ball in that direction."

Spoiling the Pitcher's Pitch

Try to spoil or foul off the really nasty or tough two-strike pitches. Just flick the bat and tip them back or to the side. If you can foul off a few of the pitcher's nastiest two-strike pitches, you will frustrate him. As a response a pitcher will often go to another pitch in an effort to fool you, or show you another speed or location. The new offering may be one that is more to your liking—and you can jump on it. Or, he may miss his intended location and leave you a "fatter" pitch to hit.

If a pitcher has extremely good control of his breaking pitches, move up closer to the plate. The idea here is to take away from the pitcher the possibility of his breaking ball crossing the outside corner for a called third strike. Now, you must prepare to look inside for a fastball (which may not

Allowing the ball to travel deep in the hitting zone affords the hitter more time to identify the type of pitch and its location. This reduces the chances of getting fooled.

be the pitcher's favorite pitch or location), because you've taken away the pitcher's most potent weapon. He must get you out with another pitch or another location.

GOOD RESEARCH WILL HELP BEAT THE 3–2 COUNT

The 3–2 count results in what broadcasters call "the payoff pitch." But with a little preparation and adjustment, a batter can deposit this payoff in his batting account. Proper preparation begins with observing what the pitcher has thrown to your teammates when they've reached 3–2 counts. Does the pitcher go to his fastball? Has he shown that he is willing to throw a curveball or other breaking ball? Does the pitcher have a change-up and is he willing to throw it on a 3–2 count? Observe and catalog his tendencies, his patterns. A pitcher is a creature of habit—he will do what he is comfortable doing over and over. Learn what that habit is and take advantage!

What about his pitch location? Does he tend to keep 3–2 deliveries on the outside (away) part of the plate, or low, or low and outside? Or does he come inside, trying to jam hitters? Pitchers have varying degrees of confidence in their pitches. For example, some will rely solely on the fastball when faced with a 3–2 count. If you have observed this tendency and know it to be true, the pitcher-batter advantage goes to you. You can now set up with confidence, knowing that he doesn't trust that he can throw his breaking pitch for a strike.

Is he a nibbler, that is, does he try to get his strikes on the outermost or innermost parts of the plate? Or does he come right at you, that is, does he rely more on his velocity and natural ball movement to deliver the ball over almost any part of the plate? This information is critical if you are to succeed more often than fail when the pitch count is 3–2. Gather it, store it, and use it when you've got only one strike left.

With two strikes, expand your strike zone and attack pitches that are borderline high, low, inside, or outside. No result is worse than a called third strike.

DRILL

When taking batting practice, assume your two-strike stance and employ the short, quick swing. Practice waiting and bringing the bat to the ball in a short and quick delivery. You will be surprised at how far you can drive the ball with this shortened, controlled swing.

6

LIFTING A FLY BALL WHEN A SACRIFICE FLY IS NEEDED

The 1991 World Series between the Minnesota Twins and Atlanta Braves was one of the greatest ever played. This Fall Classic extended seven games, five of which were decided by one run. Kirby Puckett forced a seventh and final game by clubbing a solo home run off Charlie Liebrandt in the bottom of the eleventh inning of Game 6.

The drama continued in Game 7 as the score remained deadlocked at 0–0 through nine innings of play. Twins pitcher Jack Morris pitched his tenth consecutive scoreless frame in the top of the inning, and Minnesota came to bat in the bottom of the tenth with hopes of giving the home crowd a reason to celebrate. Dan Gladden led the inning off with a bloop double, and advanced to third base on Chuck Knoblauch's sacrifice bunt. Braves reliever Alejandro Peña intentionally walked the next two batters to load the bases, setting the stage for left-handed pinch hitter Gene Larkin.

Larkin's job was simple, or so it seemed. With the infield playing in, he needed to hit a fly ball to the outfield deep enough to score Gladden from third base. Larkin dug his spikes into the batter's box, read the pitch from Peña, and sent a fly ball to left field over the head of the drawn-in out-fielder. Gladden scored easily, giving the Twins the decisive Game 7 victory and their second world championship in five years. Here is what Larkin had to say about his epic moment in baseball history: "I'd been watching [Alejandro] Peña throw all series, and he was going after everybody with high fastballs in the strike zone. I pretty much knew he was going to throw me something hard, high, and tight, or high and away. I'd always been a low-ball hitter, but in that situation I could have grounded into a double play and the game would have continued. If that first pitch was low, I probably would have taken the first pitch. But fortunately it was up and it was an ideal pitch to hit."

Larkin's approach seems very simplistic, but it is the single most important factor in successfully lifting a fly ball in a sacrifice fly situation. Get a pitch that is *up* in the strike zone. It's the easiest way to lift the ball in the air.

Getting the Ball in the Air

To hit a fly ball, the bat must contact the ball below its equator, or at a point in its lower half. This projects the ball upward. A pitch that is belt-high or even higher gives you the best chance of hitting the bottom half of the ball.

Low strikes coax batters into hitting ground balls. Because the bat starts up near your shoulders, it's difficult to catch the lower half of the ball with the barrel on pitches low in the strike zone. The tendency is to hit the top half of the ball, which produces sinking line drives and ground balls.

Pitch selection is key to driving the ball in the air to the outfield. Force the pitcher to throw the ball up in the zone by restraining yourself from swinging at low pitches. Wait for one above the thighs and give that baby a ride.

Here are a few other pointers that can help you accomplish your goal. A high strike is what you're looking for, but if the pitcher doesn't give it to you, you'll have to take matters into your own hands.

Lower Your Hands

Lowering your hands in your stance helps you to lift the ball. The lower the position from which your hands initiate the swing, the easier it is to attack the ball with a low, level swing path. A low-to-level swing path increases your chance of hitting the bottom of the ball. Try lowering your hands two or three inches to hit a fly ball.

One of the greatest home run hitters of all time, Mark McGwire, held his hands lower than most power hitters. And when Big Mac got a hold of one, it didn't just travel far, but extremely high as well. With his hands held low, McGwire contacted the lower half of the ball with regularity.

Lowering your hands can make it easier to lift the ball in sacrifice fly situations.

A Slightly Ascending Swing

Because you want to hit the lower half of the ball, allow your swing path to ascend slightly as it fires through the hitting zone. With the bat angled a few degrees downward, it gives the barrel a better chance of catching the ball just below its center. Your natural instincts guide your bat toward the middle of the ball, so if the hands allow the barrel to dip just a bit, you'll crack a fly ball every time.

Hit Through the Ball

Always hit through the ball. As the bat meets the ball, keep the bat on its swing path and drive through the ball. Make believe you're hitting two baseballs—the baseball you see and one directly behind it. If you roll your wrists prematurely and break up into your follow-through too soon, you'll raise the barrel of the bat and clip the top of the ball. Instead of a long fly ball served with an RBI attached to it, you'll hit a routine ground ball and fail to get the job done. Keep the bat on plane and hit through the baseball.

Use Your Legs on Low Strikes

Good pitchers keep their pitches at the knees in run-scoring situations. In the major leagues, there are middle relief pitchers who are called "ground ball specialists." By throwing low strikes or pitches that sink, they induce batters to hit the ball on the ground. Teams carry them on their rosters just to face hitters in this situation. They help their team out of jams by getting hitters to hit the top of the ball and not allowing them to drive the ball to the outfield.

As a hitter, you've got to work with what the pitcher gives you. To drive a low strike in the air, use your legs to lower your body to the ball. Lowering your body allows you to maintain a level swing path on low strikes. Attempting to hit low strikes by dropping the barrel to the ball manufactures three consistent results: 1) a ground ball, 2) a short pop fly or foul ball, 3) or a swing and miss. None of these outcomes is favorable to your offense. Drive your legs downward and get the bat on a level plane with the ball.

Move up in the Batter's Box

Moving up in the box is another simple adjustment that increases your chances of hitting the ball in the air. By drawing a line from the pitcher's

The best way to increase your chances of hitting the ball in the air is to swing at pitches up in the strike zone.

release point to the catcher's glove, you'll notice that a fastball descends on its path to home plate. Standing farther up in the box gives you a greater chance of meeting the ball at a point slightly higher than if you were standing at the rear of the box.

In addition, moving up in the box allows you to hit a breaking ball before or in the early stage of its break. Because a breaking ball drops or slides downward, it becomes increasingly difficult to drive it in the air if you hit it near the back of the batter's box. Move up and catch it before it breaks.

Developing into a hitter who is capable of driving the ball in the air in run-scoring situations increases your value to a ball club. Twins manager Tom Kelly had enough faith in Gene Larkin to send him up to pinch-hit in a crucial moment during Game 7 of the World Series. Larkin came through in the clutch and will forever be linked to a heroic moment in baseball history.

7

HITTING TO THE RIGHT SIDE (WITH A RUNNER ON SECOND BASE)

"Think about deliberately hitting the ball to that area that stretches all the way from the shortstop's left to the right-field line. Over time you will be able to hit the hole between first and second when the first base-man comes in to play close to the bag or you will be able to hit the ball over the second baseman's head."

—CHARLEY LAU

Have you ever witnessed this scenario during a baseball game? The first batter of an inning strokes a double. The next batter hits a ground ball to the second baseman and is thrown out at first base. Upon returning to the dugout, the batter is congratulated by his teammates. They're giving him high fives and pats on the back as if he'd just smacked a home run. Confused? Well, there is no reason to be. That second batter just made a significant, unselfish contribution to his team.

By hitting the ball to the right side of second base, the base runner was able to advance to third base. With the leadoff hitter now standing on third base with one out, the third batter of the inning only needs to put the ball in play (assuming the infield plays at regular depth) to score the run. The second batter sacrificed his hopes of getting a hit by intentionally grounding the ball to second base. That's called teamwork, and it's a method of manufacturing runs.

Learning the Technique

The technique used for hitting the ball to the right side of second base is completely different for right-handed hitters than it is for left-handed hitters. The ability to do so, however, is born from the same roots. Becoming adept at this skill requires excellent bat control. Here's how to get the job done from each side of the plate.

Right-Handed Batters

To hit the ball to the opposite field, two things have to happen: 1) The ball must travel deep into the hitting zone—let it get to you. 2) The angle of the bat must face the opposite-field side—keep the barrel back. Picture your hands as the center of a clock and the bat pointing to four o'clock on the face. Making contact deep in the hitting zone with the barrel angled toward the second base side will produce balls hit to the right side every time.

Allowing the barrel to trail the hands and minimizing hip rotation are key elements to hitting the ball to the right side for right-handed hitters.

The top hand has the critical role of keeping the barrel above the ball. If the top hand is lazy, the barrel of the bat will dip beneath the equator of the ball and produce a pop fly.

On pitches thrown to the outside corner, your job is easy. Hit the ball with your normal swing. Let the ball travel to the rear portion of home plate, minimize your hip rotation, and swing the bat level. Because you're looking to hit a ground ball in this situation, make sure the barrel stays above the ball as you swing the bat. One way to do this is to keep your spine as vertical as possible during the stride and rotation. Standing straight levels out your swing plane and creates more line drives and ground balls.

Smart pitchers, however, will realize your objective at the plate and counter your intentions. They'll throw pitches over the middle and inside portions of the plate in hopes of making you pull the pitch, so you've got to alter your natural swing slightly to carry out your obligations to the team.

On middle and inside strikes, the two basic rules to hitting the ball to the opposite field still apply. The ball has to travel back in the hitting zone and you've got to angle the bat toward the second base side. To do this,

Notice how the hips face second base after contact has been made. This positioning keeps the shoulders from flying open and prevents hits to the pull side of the infield.

allow the lead arm (or bottom hand) to dominate your swing, which keeps the barrel back so it trails the hands. This is often referred to as an "inside-out swing." Don't let your top hand take over and fire the barrel in front of home plate. This produces ground balls to the shortstop side of the infield.

Quiet your hips (allow for minimal rotation, that is, your belly button should not rotate past an imaginary line from the pitcher to the plate). If you fully rotate, the hands move forward, as will your point of contact. Hitting the ball out front produces balls that travel to the pull side. Also, keep the barrel raised above the ball. Hitters have a tendency to dip their barrel when executing an inside-out swing. The last thing you want is to hit a shallow pop fly.

Left-Handed Batters

The target is the same for left-handed hitters, but their approach to the ball is the exact opposite of the method used by right-handed hitters.

Getting the barrel of the bat out early creates pull hits for left-handed batters.

Instead of allowing the ball to travel back over home plate and using a bottom-hand dominant swing, left-handed hitters have to contact the ball out in front of home plate and let the top hand control the swing.

To pull the ball, the barrel has to get to the ball early and be angled to the pull side of the field. This is accomplished by swinging sooner, not swinging harder. An earlier swing is the end result of a chain of events that begins with the stride. Stride toward the pitcher a little sooner than normal and move your hands back to the launch or loaded position. Getting set in the launch position sooner allows you to initiate your forward swing earlier and gives you more time to get the barrel out in front of home plate as the ball arrives.

As you begin your forward swing, feel your top hand thrust the barrel forward. The bat will angle itself toward the pull side of the field and project batted balls in that direction. Keep the barrel slightly raised to produce ground balls.

Anticipate a fastball when you're at bat in this situation. If the pitcher throws an off-speed pitch, you can always slow your hands down and still hit an adequate ground ball to the right side. If you look for an off-speed pitch and the pitcher throws a fastball, you'll be late swinging, which eliminates any chance of hitting the ball to the right side.

Keep in mind that this approach and swing is to carry out the job at hand. It deviates from your normal hitting approach.

Avoiding the Bunt Sign

Good hitters never like to see the sacrifice bunt sign flashed when they're standing at home plate. Even though they accept the task and do their best to lay down an efficient bunt, they would much rather be swinging the bat.

Exhibiting good bat control can convince your coach or manager to think twice before flashing the bunt sign. If he's confident in your ability to hit the ball to the right and advance the runner, there's no need to sacrifice an out. Your main objective remains the same—move the runner to third base. Swinging the bat, however, offers a chance to hit the ball through the hole on the right side. Perhaps luck is on your side and your attempt to advance the runner will turn into a base hit.

Become efficient at hitting to the right side and gain the opportunity to swing the bat. Hitting away, after all, is why you carry a bat.

8

THE SLASH

"Offer to bunt; then pull the bat back and take a full swing. Just put the ball in play. It's very effective if you know what you're doing."
—TONY GWYNN

Ty Cobb was one of the most feared players to ever play baseball. The type of fear he instilled in his opponents is twofold. Pitchers dreaded facing Cobb because of his exceptional prowess at the plate. He was a very astute, patient hitter who stung the ball with precision, lacing line drives through the infield with historic consistency. He was also a menace on the base paths, combining exceptional speed with unparalleled aggressiveness. To say that he was a distraction when he reached base would understate the impact his presence had on pitchers.

But Cobb was also one of the darkest, most volatile figures to ever play the game. His temperamental and sometimes violent behavior invoked trepidation among opposing players. Cobb verbally badgered players and frequently spiked basemen by sliding with his sharpened metal cleats facing upward.

One facet of Cobb's game combined his intelligence, athletic talents, and competitive ferocity. He was a master of the slash play and kept cornermen on their toes and heels, but rarely on the balls of their feet.

Cobb was an accomplished bunter and with his great speed, often bunted for base hits. But he used this skill to his advantage even when swinging the bat. Cobb once said, "The threat in a bunt is a marvelous weapon." He was known to bunt two or three times in a row to lure the infielders in, then fake a bunt, pull his bat back, and drive the ball straight at one of them. It may sound savage, but slashing is extremely effective and a tactic that is accepted and still utilized in the game today.

Use the pivot method when showing bunt. Use a convincing presentation to sell the defense.

Executing the Slash Play

The slash is used in sacrifice bunt situations. With the first and third basemen creeping in toward home plate in anticipation of a bunt, the batter pivots on the balls of his feet to give the impression he's bunting. As the pitcher breaks into his delivery, the batter pulls the bat back and takes a short swing at the pitch. A ball hit on the ground is almost certain to be a base hit. When executed properly the batter reaches base, the base runners advance, and no out is sacrificed.

There are two accepted methods of sacrifice bunting: squaring around and pivoting. When executing the slash play, use the pivot method. Move a step closer to home plate and as the pitcher moves to the set position, pivot on your rear foot so the toe points to the pitcher. Slide your bottom hand halfway up the handle and your right hand up to the barrel of the bat. Bend at the knees and push the bat out toward the pitcher as if you're preparing to bunt the ball. It's important to convince the defense that you intend to bunt the ball. If they notice you're just setting them up, they'll retreat to their positions.

As the pitcher lifts his leg and then breaks his hands, pull the bat back and pivot your rear foot back to its original position. Slide your top hand down the bat until it touches your bottom hand. Your bottom hand stays put, so your hands should be choked up three or four inches on the bat. Choking up helps ensure contact and makes it easier to hit the ball on the ground. Move the bat back to your customary stance position and hit the pitch on the ground if it's a strike.

Get It on the Ground

Your primary goal is to hit the ball on the ground in fair territory. By accomplishing that simple goal, you're almost guaranteed a base hit. Consider the positioning of the infielders. The first and third basemen are charging forward to field a bunt. Once you pull the bat back to hit, they'll either dive for cover or be positioned too close to you to field a hit. The second baseman is running over to cover first base, so nearly the entire

Once the pitcher begins his delivery, simply pivot back to your original stance position. Keep your hands choked up on the bat to ensure contact and improve bat control.

Keep your barrel above the ball and hit the ball on the ground. Hitting the ball on the ground nearly guarantees a base hit when slashing.

right side of the infield is open. The shortstop is running over to cover second base, so nearly the entire left side of the field is open. The only ways to make an out are to hit the ball back to the pitcher, hit the ball directly at the moving second baseman or shortstop, or pop the ball up. Other than those three areas, the hitting lanes are vast.

Under most circumstances in amateur baseball, bunting, stealing, and slashing plays are instituted by the coach. If the coach puts on a play, your job is to execute that play, not to question it. There is one situation, however, where you *should* alter the play call to counter a defensive scheme. With runners on first and second and nobody out, your coach may flash the sacrifice bunt signal. As a general rule, use the pivot method when bunting in this situation. The pivot method allows you to call an audible at the plate if necessary. As you square around, watch the movement by the infielders. If they are in a "rotation coverage," slash automatically. Rotation coverage means that the first and third basemen are charging aggressively toward home plate. The second baseman covers first base and the shortstop breaks early (before the pitcher lifts his leg) to cover third base. (The second base bag is left open.) In short, the entire middle of the infield is left wide open to hit the ball through. Pull the bat back and slash.

Cobb may have been crazy on and off the field, but the man did accumulate 4,191 career hits and still holds the all-time record for career batting average (.367). Add a weapon to your own offensive arsenal and become a proficient slasher. It's an easy way to get to first base.

9

PUSH BUNT FOR A BASE HIT

"When you push the ball between the pitcher and first baseman, those guys have to get it together quickly to decide who is going to cover the bag. You want to capitalize on that moment of confusion. If there's a split second of indecision, you'll beat the throw."

—TONY GWYNN

By the late 1970s, the Philadelphia Phillies had developed a strong nucleus of homegrown talent in Mike Schmidt, Larry Bowa, Bob Boone, and Greg Luzinksi. Expectations of a dynasty ran high, but the Phils could not seem to make the leap from a great group of players to a championship team. They lost to the Cincinnati Reds in the 1976 National League Championship Series, and followed with consecutive NLCS setbacks to the Los Angeles Dodgers in 1977 and 1978.

In 1980, the Phillies returned to the postseason and were embroiled in an epic battle with the Houston Astros. Three of the first four games were decided in extra innings, setting up a decisive Game 5 at the Houston Astrodome. The Astros built a 5–2 lead, and with Nolan Ryan in total control of the game entering the eighth inning, a Fall Classic invitation for Houston seemed imminent.

Bowa led off the eighth inning with a punch-shot base hit to left-center field. Boone followed with an infield single off of Ryan's glove. With runners on first and second and nobody out, left-handed pinch hitter Greg Gross stepped to the plate. A sacrifice bunt was undoubtedly in the thoughts of each club. Several factors, however, kept the sacrifice bunt play from being a foregone conclusion. With Ryan throwing fastballs in the mid-to-upper 90-mph range, bunting the ball effectively was no easy task. The Astroturf surface would also make it difficult to have "touch" on the bunt. A ball bunted too hard could initiate a rally-killing double play. Lastly, the Phillies were down by three runs. With only two innings to play, they were not at liberty to give away outs. A sacrifice bunt would advance both base runners, but they needed three men to cross home plate and not just two.

As Ryan started his delivery to home plate, Gross showed no signs of squaring around, which kept third baseman Enos Cabell at bay. As the pitch was released, Gross dropped his hands, started his feet toward first base, and pushed a perfect bunt down the third-base line. The hard-throwing Ryan, who falls off toward the first base side in his follow-through, had no chance of the making the play. Cabell was positioned too deep to field the ball in time, and Gross legged out a critical bunt base hit.

The rest is history. Ryan walked Pete Rose to force in a run and was chased from the game. Del Unser tied the game with a double, and series Most Valuable Player Manny Trillo put the Phils ahead 7–5 with a two-run triple. It took the Phillies extra innings to prevail in Game 5, and they went on to defeat the Kansas City Royals in six games to secure their elusive first world championship.

Several players made significant contributions along the way, but the bunt by Gross may have been the key to unlocking the vault holding the World Series trophy.

The push bunt differs from a sacrifice bunt and a drag bunt. A push bunt is used as a means to reach first base safely—to get a base hit. Sacrifice bunts are executed to advance base runners—to sacrifice your at-bat for the team. Push bunts are balls bunted to the opposite field, whereas drag bunts are directed toward the pull side of the infield. The push bunt is a very effective weapon if it's performed properly and at the right time.

The Push Bunt—Right-Handed Batters

If you're a right-handed batter, take your customary stance at the plate. Do not move up in the box or closer to the plate as you may for a sacrifice bunt. Your goal is to bunt the ball to the first base side, so you want the ball to be away from you and to let it travel deep near the back of home plate.

As the pitcher starts his delivery, remain in your stance. Deception is key to a successful push bunt, so give the impression that you're planning

When push bunting from the right side, drop your rear foot back and square your shoulders to first base. As you bunt the ball, push off your left foot and begin sprinting to first base.

to hit away. Once the pitcher arrives at his release point, drop your rear foot back and lower your hands. Keep the barrel up and your front shoulder closed. Slide your right hand up the barrel of the bat and move your left hand up to the top of the handle. Angle the barrel back so it faces the second base position. Push your arms out slightly and track the incoming pitch with both eyes.

Meet the ball with your bat. As the ball contacts the bat, your feet should begin moving toward first base. This is an advanced skill that requires excellent timing. The advantage is that you'll have momentum going toward first base as you bunt the ball.

Where to Bunt the Ball

Two factors dictate where your target location is on a push bunt. The first is infield positioning and the second is with which arm the pitcher throws the ball. If the first baseman is playing very deep, use the first-base line. Bunt the ball hard enough so the catcher can't make the play, soft enough to foil the first baseman, and close enough to the foul line to take the pitcher out of the equation. For this situation, the perfect place for a push bunt is one where if no defensive player were to touch the ball, it would come to rest approximately 10 feet short of the first base bag.

With a left-handed pitcher on the mound and the second baseman playing deep, take a different approach. Bunt the ball firmly toward the second base position. It has to be bunted hard enough to get past the pitcher. Because a southpaw will fall off to the third base side, he's not as quick to field balls to his left.

Once the ball gets past the pitcher, it becomes an extremely difficult play for the second baseman. Even if he gets to the ball in time, he's got to field it cleanly and throw the ball across his body in one motion. Accomplishing this feat while coming off a dead sprint forward is a pretty tall order.

The Push Bunt—Left-Handed Batters

From the left-hand side of the plate, the footwork is a little different. As the pitch is released, take a small step toward home plate with your rear foot. Lower your hands (keeping the barrel raised), slide your hands up the bat, and angle it toward the shortstop position.

The reason you take an initial step toward home plate with the rear foot is to move yourself a little closer to home plate, and to keep you from opening up your shoulders and leaving for first prematurely. Left-handed hitters have a tendency to take the first step with their front foot in the direction of first base. This immediately opens your body and pulls you away from home plate. Remember, when push bunting, you've got to let the ball get deep in the hitting zone. If your body is pulling toward first base as the pitch arrives, you'll contact the ball out in front of home plate, and in most cases, bunt the ball back to the pitcher. Remind yourself to stay closed and patient.

Keep the barrel above the ball and facing the left side of the infield. Track the pitch with both eyes and move to the ball with your hands and feet. Once the ball contacts the bat, take off for first base.

Where to Bunt the Ball

Much like the right-handed push bunt, the defense dictates your target area. If the third baseman is playing very deep, use the third-base line. Bunt the ball hard enough so the catcher is unable to make a play, soft enough to eliminate the third baseman, and close enough to the foul line

Because the ball has to travel deep to direct the ball to third base, left-handed hitters can wait until the last instant to show bunt. Keep the barrel above the ball and push off your right foot as you bunt the ball. Remember, if your bunt is going to miss its intended target, make sure it misses to the foul side.

to leave the pitcher hopeless. The perfect place to bunt the ball is so it comes to rest approximately 20 feet from third base.

Facing a right-handed pitcher, check to see how far back the shortstop is playing. If he's deep or cheating toward second base, bunt the ball firmly enough to get past the pitcher. The shortstop will have a long run in to field the ball followed by a long throw across the diamond (on the run). A right-handed pitcher falls off to the first base side and has limited range on bunts to his right.

Get the Right Pitch

You are not executing a bunt-and-run play, so make sure you get a good pitch to bunt. The perfect pitch to push-bunt is a fastball up in the strike zone and out over the plate. Inside strikes are very difficult to handle when push bunting, so pull the bat back if the pitch is thrown in on your hands. Low strikes are also tough because you're trying to bunt the ball with some momentum. Look for pitches above the belt, and let the low strikes pass.

Because a successful push bunt relies heavily on timing, off-speed pitches are best left alone. The decreased velocity makes it difficult to wait, and you'll risk bunting the ball too close to the pitcher. If you identify the pitch as a breaking ball, let it go.

FIELDING

Introduction

Pitching and defense win baseball games. The New York Yankees, winners of four World Series championships since 1996, have proven that profoundly. Prodigious home run totals and offensive statistical chaos may provide footage for highlight shows, but its impact on winning baseball games rides in the backseat. Minimize the number of earned runs the opposition scores and you possess the main ingredient for baking up a batch of victories.

The majority of baseball fans outside of the state of Georgia groan in anguish when the Atlanta Braves qualify for the postseason. Since 1991, the Braves have won their division title every year. Every year! That is an incredible run, especially when considering the advent of free agency. Their formula for success has been very simple. Their pitchers throw the ball over the plate (with discernment), forcing the hitters to swing the bat and put the ball in play. The fielders catch the ball and record outs routinely. This strategy keeps pitch counts down, keeps runners off the base paths, and minimizes the number of runs throughout a game. The offense supplies enough production to score more runs than their defense allows.

That groan in anguish from fans is heard because the Braves are not a spectacular team. They're not explosive or majestic, but rather efficient and consistent. They're a professional baseball organization that knows what it takes to win, and should not be held in contempt by reason of continuous success.

Pitching is the key to winning games, without question. During their 10-year run (they lost a season in 1994 due to the strike) the Braves' pitching staff led the National League in earned run average every year but two. In 1991 they were third in the league (3.49), and in 1996 they were second in the league (3.53). Pitching, however, can only travel as far as its defense allows it to. Once the ball is put in play, the pitcher becomes powerless to impact the play's outcome. Proficient defensive play in baseball is what offensive linemen are to football—absolutely essential, yet largely unnoticed.

Standing Above the Rest

Fielding the routine plays is a characteristic of every good defensive player. Because you're reading this book, it's understood that you are capable of consistently making the routine plays. The types of defensive plays discussed in this section are those that separate the good defensive players and the great ones. A ball in the shortstop hole, a slow roller to third, or an over-the-shoulder catch in the outfield are plays that not only tack an out on the scoreboard, but can also shift the momentum of a game.

Just as is the case with making routine plays, technique is vitally important to executing advanced fielding plays. Many of these plays are performed on the move or on the run. Employing the correct technique provides you the best opportunity for balance, throwing accuracy, and arm strength. Take the time to learn the proper movements and then practice the execution until it becomes ingrained in your muscle memory.

Preparation and anticipation are also important to making advanced plays. For example, turning a 6-4-3 double play (shortstop to second base to first base) is initiated by the shortstop fielding the ball and throwing to second base for the force-out. While an accurate and timely feed is necessary, the turn made by the second baseman is what makes or breaks the play. The foundation of a good turn is proper footwork. The second baseman must address the speed and location of the hit to determine what type of turn to use. Is it to the shortstop's backhand? If so, he'll have to come across the bag. Is the ball hit directly to the shortstop? If so, he'll use the back of the base to make the turn. Whatever the case may be, the second baseman must get to the bag quickly and decide immediately what type of turn to use to have a chance at turning the double play. It's a combination of mental awareness and physical ability.

Take the time to learn the fundamentals of these advanced fielding plays. They are not as complex as they appear to be when they're approached and performed correctly. Focus on the basic steps and you'll generate favorable results with greater ease and consistency.

10

OUTFIELDER GOING BACK ON A FLY BALL

There is an old cliché in baseball that says, "It's easier to come in on a fly ball than to go back." It's true, and that's why outfielders often play deeper rather than shallower. They're afraid that a batter will hit a fly ball safely between them and the fence or wall behind them. Darryl Strawberry, when he played for the New York Mets, was notorious for playing every hitter in the same place, a well-worn area that was dubbed "the Strawberry Patch" because Strawberry spent so much time in it.

But to become an accomplished outfielder you must learn how to go back on a fly ball. When you do, you will become confident of being able to retreat and catch a ball behind you. Thus, you can play shallower and catch more of the balls that flare just over the infield. Here is how to play balls that are hit over your head.

Chasing Down Fly Balls

First, learn to anticipate the long fly ball by closely watching the swing of each batter. A more forceful, and thus more powerful, swing is more likely to send a ball over your head toward the wall or fence. A shorter, choppier swing is more likely to produce a fly ball in front of you.

Second, practice taking off even before the sound of the crack of the bat reaches you. Light travels faster than sound, so learn to read the swing even before you hear it. With repetition and careful practice, you should be able to judge the distance a ball will travel during the first few feet after it leaves the bat. Watch the arc. Long fly balls leave the bat at an angle of

When the ball is hit over your head, your first step is a drop step. This movement opens your hips to where the ball is traveling and allows you to run to the point of the ball's descent.

approximately 45 degrees. Turn and run to the spot at which you've judged the ball will fall. On balls hit straight overhead and behind you turn with your glove side facing toward the bat, glance up, and sprint to the spot where you think the ball will descend.

As you run look back quickly at the wall, then back up at the ball, and then concentrate on its descent. If you are close to the wall and have enough time before the ball comes down, move to the wall, touch it lightly, and then drift back away from it. If you do not have enough time, put out your hand closest to the wall and feel for it until you make contact. Make sure you do not collide with the wall.

Not-So-Routine Fly Balls

Here are two other catches that you need to make if you are to become an accomplished player: 1) the curving ball, 2) the ball nearing the fence.

Do not drift; instead, turn your back and run. Turning your back to the ball enables you to cover more ground in less time.

Glance up to find the ball. If you have time, circle around it so you can catch the ball over your throwing shoulder with your momentum moving toward the infield.

Playing the Curving Ball

Fly balls hit near the foul line will usually curve toward the foul line. The higher and deeper a ball is hit, the more it will curve toward the foul line.

Naturally, the direction and force of a strong wind will either increase or decrease the curve of the ball, but it will always curve toward the foul line.

When playing left or right field you must always anticipate the curve of the ball. Start adjusting immediately rather than running along with the ball and then suddenly discovering that it is curving and starting to think, "Uh-oh, I better change direction." By then it may be too late.

The experienced outfielder will overanticipate the curve of the ball toward the foul line. It's a form of insurance. If you misjudge the extent of the curve, you will still be able to either slow down and wait for the ball to come to you, or go back slightly and meet the curve.

If you underanticipate the curve of the ball, you will have to keep running to catch up to the ball as it curves away.

If a curving ball is hit over your head, turn in the direction of the foul line and go back for the ball, as it will always curve in that direction. With your body facing the foul line (as you go back) you can keep the ball in view at all times.

If you turn away from the foul line as you go back, you will have to turn toward the foul line as the ball begins to curve—and you will momentarily (at least) lose sight of the ball.

Playing the Fence

On a high fly ball headed for a fence, you must judge the flight and then sprint to the fence. Once you find the fence (reach out with your closest hand) you can turn, relocate the ball, and make any adjustment needed to make the catch.

Many outfielders use the arm nearest the fence to help locate it. Of course, a warning track is also helpful to let you know you are approaching the fence.

Inexperienced outfielders often are afraid to take their eyes off the ball. They will "tiptoe" toward the fence and "feel" for it cautiously. As a result, they will sometimes fail to catch high fly balls that are not even close to the fence.

A line-drive fly ball to the fence is much more difficult to catch than a high fly ball. You will only have time for a glance at the fence before hav-

On balls hit deep to the fence, use your throwing arm to reach out and find the fence.

ing to relocate the ball. Thus, you may be unable to get back to the fence and get balanced to make the catch.

It takes a lot of work (and a lot of courage) to run full speed toward a fence. But, with experience and proper practice, it can be accomplished.

Playing a ball off the fence is another skill that requires a lot of concentration. Many outfielders have trouble with this play because they take their eyes off the ball and look toward the infield too quickly, or because they stop and reach for the ball rather than get directly above the ball to pick it up.

Some outfielders also have trouble getting the throw away quickly, and that problem is usually caused by improper footwork. Here is the proper technique.

When a ball rebounds off the fence to your throwing side, run to the ball, step past it with your right foot (right-hand thrower), and pick the ball up with your bare hand.

The ball should be directly between the feet when it is picked up. Make a quick crow hop to get on balance and get the body moving in the direction of the throw. Then make a strong overhand throw.

If the ball is hit to your glove side, run quickly to the ball and step past the ball with your right foot, turning your back toward home plate (right-handed thrower), which should put your body directly over the ball.

Use your glove to block the sun. When the ball is hit, block the sun with your glove *first*, and then find the ball.

Pick the ball up with your bare hand and make a quick reverse-pivot to turn the body in the direction of the throw. **Note:** be careful not to turn too far and open up the body too much when executing the reverse-pivot.

A Fast and Efficient Delivery

Make a quick crow hop and a good overhand throw to complete the play. Get the arm up and make an overhand throw.

Be quick in getting to the rebound and making the throw to the relay man, but be sure to use the proper footwork and throwing form in making the play. Sloppy execution causes errors—you will miss picking up the ball cleanly or will make a poor throw in your haste to get rid of it.

All outfielders should be required to master these skills, but they are particularly important to the left and right fielders, as they more often have to deal with the balls curving toward the foul line.

They are also more likely to be looking into the sun in the afternoon. Not too many baseball fields have the sun in center field, and since right and left fields have the shortest fence distances, those players have to be more concerned about being able to play a ball hit near the fence.

The difference between an average defensive outfielder and an outstanding one lies in the ability to make these difficult catches.

BALL IN THE SUN

All of us have seen an outfielder staggering around under a ball coming out of the sun, and ending up with the ball falling to the ground or, even worse, hitting the outfielder on the chest, head, or back. It can be a very tough play, but there are some techniques that can help you catch a ball in the sun.

The outfielder should not hesitate to shift his position slightly anytime the sun is directly in line with his view of the hitter. It is certainly better to be a couple of steps "out of position" and be able to see the ball clearly as it comes off the bat, than to be in "perfect position" and not be able to see the ball because of the glare.

Too many outfielders lock into a position—set up in the same spot for every hitter without regard to the pitcher, the hitter, or the position of the sun.

If the sun is directly behind the hitter and you cannot see the ball coming off the bat, move your position. A couple of steps off to the side will allow you to see the ball as it is hit and perhaps get a jump on the ball.

Even after the ball is hit, it may be helpful to move to the side a step or two if the ball is hit directly in line with the sun. The new angle may enable you to pick up the ball and make the catch. If you have sunglasses, use them.

Having sunglasses available and using them are often two different things. Many players don't like to wear sunglasses and never practice with them or even use them in games. But you should wear them in practice, intrasquad games, and regular games until you become comfortable using them.

Flip-down sunglasses should be worn in the upper position until a ball is hit into the sun and their use is required. The outfielder must then simply tap the bill of his cap or hit the tab on the side of the lens to flip the glasses down. This technique can be learned in a few practice sessions.

Some outfielders prefer to wear standard sunglasses rather than the flip-down variety. These sunglasses are quite acceptable and require no special training. You can put them on at the start of the game and leave them on for the entire game or until it clouds up and they are no longer needed.

Sometimes even the use of sunglasses is not enough on balls hit right into the sun. The outfielder must also learn to shade his eyes with his glove. The glove will provide more shade and it can successfully shield the eyes either by holding it close to the face or by extending the arm.

Flip down the glasses, shade your eyes (and protect your face at the same time) with the glove, and keep looking. Even if the ball is "lost" in the sun, the ball will eventually emerge and you should be able to catch it at the last split second.

11

OUTFIELDER FIELDING A GROUND BALL AND MAKING THE THROW

The typical defensive responsibilities of an outfielder are pretty simple. If the ball is hit in the air, try to catch it before it hits the ground. If the ball does hit the ground—whether it be a fly ball, line drive, or ground ball—field it and throw it back to the infield.

Every so often, however, an outfielder gets involved in a spine-tingling play. A courageous or wily base runner may act on thoughts of stretching his luck to reach the next base. It's the outfielder's job to field the ball cleanly, quickly get into throwing position, and rifle a strike to the base under attack. Learn to make this play correctly and base runners will think twice about pushing their luck on the base paths.

Know the Game Situation

The first step to making this play is to know which base to throw the ball to before it's hit. Deciding as you make the play is not the best method of execution. With runners on base, you'll have two or sometimes three options as to where the ball should be thrown. Tell yourself (before the pitch) where you're throwing the ball if the ball is hit in specific areas.

Here is an example of a game scenario and what the outfielder should review in anticipation of the ball being hit in his direction.

The game is in the fourth inning, your team is leading by two runs, and a runner is on second base with one out. You're playing left field. If the ball is hit on the ground or a line between the shortstop and third base hole, charge the ball, field it, and throw home. If the ball takes you a significant distance to your right or left, field the ball and throw it to second base to keep the batter from reaching second base. He is not in scoring position and the double play is still in order.

What is a significant distance? If you have to run more than four or five strides laterally before charging forward, you won't have a chance of throwing the runner out at home plate. If it's only a step or two to either side and the ball is hit hard, you'll still have a play. The location and speed of the hit are the determining factors, but review each circumstance ahead of time to avoid any hesitation.

Aligning Your Approach

Once the ball is hit, align yourself directly behind the ball before charging full-steam ahead. On a ball hit slightly to your left, circle forward and to your left until you, the ball, and your target are in a direct line with each other. By aligning yourself with the ball and target, you can sprint straight to the ball and be in position to make an immediate throw. The momentum built by running directly to the ball also adds strength to your throw.

At times, you have to run laterally a few steps to align yourself with the base you're throwing to. Do your best to align yourself with the target first, and then charge the ball.

Fielding the ball at an angle to your target adds time and reduces the strength of your throw. It forces you to shift your body into alignment before throwing the ball, adds time to your release, and gives the base runner extra steps. (Remember, for each additional step you take in the outfield to release the ball, the base runner gains two steps.) Also, shifting your body in another direction wipes out the forward momentum built up during your approach.

Get behind the ball and then sprint to it as quickly as possible. It will produce stronger, more accurate throws that are released sooner rather than later.

Making the Play

The base runners are running at top speed, and so should you on this play. Use the "do or die" method to field the ball. Run as fast as you can to the ball to 1) field it as quickly as possible, and 2) shorten the distance between you and your target point. As you approach the ball, extend your glove out to the ball. Bend at the waist and reach down so your glove touches the ground.

If you're right-handed, field the ball just out in front and to the left of your left foot. The ball is fielded as the left foot is taking a stride forward.

Bend at the waist and reach out with your glove to field the ball in front of your glove-side foot.

As you transfer the ball from glove to hand, take a crow hop. It will increase the strength of your throw.

Left-handers field the ball in front of and outside of their right foot. Catching the ball is performed as you're on the run. Slow down enough to bend at the waist and get your glove to the ground, but do not stop or "hit the brakes" as you field the ball. Momentum aids your throw, so you've got to sustain it.

After you field the ball off your glove-side foot, take a crow hop. Jump off your glove-side foot, align your shoulders to the target, and transfer the ball from glove to hand. Land on your rear foot, stride, and throw. This entire sequence happens as your body moves forward.

The breakdown of footwork is as follows for a right-handed player:

- Sprint to the ball and bend over to field it as your left foot takes a step forward.

- Field the ball just outside of and to the left of your left foot.

- Take an immediate crow hop; leap off of your left foot, align your shoulders with the target, and transfer the ball into your throwing hand.

- Turn and land with your right foot perpendicular to the target; then stride square to the target with your left foot.

- Throw the ball directly to the chest of your cutoff man.

Keep Your Throws on a Line

When you're attempting to throw a base runner out, keep the ball down and on a straight line to the target. Long, looping throws take extra time. As your teammate stands and waits for the ball to drop from the sky, the runner is eating up ground. When throwing to second or third base, aim to throw the ball on a line to the baseman's glove. On throws home, aim for the chest of your cutoff man.

If you can't reach your target in the air, throw it on one bounce. It gets to the base faster than a high, soaring throw, and also gives your teammate a greater chance to field the ball and apply a tag (or throw to another base). A throw that sails over the head of your teammate leaves him no chance to field the ball.

IMPROVING YOUR THROWS FROM THE OUTFIELD

To build arm strength, stretch the distance of your throws with regularity. Long-tossing is the ideal exercise for improving your arm strength. At the beginning of each practice, start by having a catch with a partner. After your arm is loose, extend the distance between you and your teammate in five-foot increments. Begin at a comfortable distance and then move back five steps every three throws. Make sure you maintain proper mechanics on each throw.

Continue to throw the ball on a straight line to the chest of your partner. Eventually, you'll be unable to reach your partner in the air on a straight line. Do not elevate the arc of your throws just to get the ball to him in the air. Instead, reach him on one bounce.

Keep track of the distance you're able to reach your partner in the air. Use it as a means to measure your improvement. The long-toss exercise, if practiced regularly, builds arm strength in a matter of days and weeks. Here are a few other tips to help strengthen your throws from the outfield.

- Drop your arm down to create a longer arm swing. Infielders are taught to pull the ball out of their glove and bring their arm straight back, like pulling the arrow back when shooting a bow. From the outfield, drop your arm down to lengthen your arm swing and increase the momentum that builds into your throw.
- Stay on top of the ball. Keep your hand and fingers on top so your wrist snaps and your fingers pull down on the seams upon release to create backspin and help the ball carry. Do not drop your arm and wrist down and throw from underneath the ball.

- Stay behind the ball. Plant and stiffen your front leg and then thrust forward with your upper body. This allows you to release the ball out in front of your body. Do not rush your upper body forward over a bent front leg. Much like a pitcher, your arm will trail behind, reducing your throwing speed and accuracy.
- Extend on each throw. Do not cut your follow-through short or fail to finish your throw. Throw through the baseball and follow through completely so that your throwing arm finishes across your opposite-side leg.

The best method of building arm strength is long-tossing. Make it a point to long-toss every day with a teammate.

12

OUTFIELDER MAKING A CATCH AND THROW WHEN RUNNER IS TAGGING UP

Game 6 of the 1975 World Series between the Cincinnati Reds and Boston Red Sox is considered by many as the greatest World Series game ever played. The image of Carlton Fisk frantically waving his arms as his twelfth inning blast soared toward the left-field foul pole is familiar to nearly every baseball fan.

Although Fisk's home run has become legendary, his extra-inning heroics would have never transpired had it not been for the throwing arm of Reds outfielder George Foster.

With the score tied at six in the bottom of the ninth inning, Boston's Denny Doyle led off with a walk and Carl Yastrzemski followed with a single. Fisk was intentionally walked and the Sox had the bases loaded with nobody out. Needing only a sacrifice fly to win the game, rookie Fred Lynn lofted a fly ball down the left-field line. Foster ran over to make the catch, and with Doyle tagging up, fired a strike to catcher Johnny Bench. Doyle was called out at the plate to complete the double play and keep the game alive. Rico Petrocelli then grounded out to third to end the inning and the Reds miraculously survived, forcing the game into extra innings.

Three innings later, Fisk launched his legendary drive off the left-field foul pole, sending the series to a seventh game. But without the clutch defensive play by Foster, the game would have ended in regulation, thus erasing Fisk's homer from history.

Making the Play

Catching a fly ball and throwing when a runner is tagging up can be a pivotal play in a baseball game. Cutting down a runner can keep a run off the scoreboard and quickly shift the momentum of the game. The two most important factors in catching a fly ball and making a throw occur before you even touch the ball. First, you must have an awareness of the situation. Where am I going to throw the ball if it's hit to a particular location? Second, you've got to get your body behind the ball so you catch it moving forward with momentum. Throws are stronger when released with forward momentum.

Awareness

With only a runner on third base, it's easy to decide where to throw the ball following the catch. Throw the ball home. With multiple base runners, however, you've got to do your homework before each pitch is thrown. For example, with runners on first and third base, the runner on first base can tag up and advance, putting himself into scoring position. You have to decide how deep is too deep for you to take a shot at the lead runner trying to score. If you have no chance, it's best to throw the ball to second base and keep the runner on first from advancing.

Depth is not the only element that factors into the equation. The ball may be hit to your right or left. After catching the ball on the run, it takes time to gather yourself and make a strong throw to home plate. Another base may be the best option. Wind can also become a factor. Throwing with the wind allows you to lengthen the distance from which you'll make an attempt to throw home. Throwing against the wind shortens that distance.

Lastly, know who is on base. Runners vary in speed. With a slow runner on third base, you may have a good chance of throwing him out. A swift runner may beat a strong throw easily, so it would be best to throw to another base.

Throwing with Forward Momentum

In sacrifice fly situations, catching the ball is not your only responsibility as an outfielder. Catch the ball in a position to make a strong throw. Once

When a runner is tagging up on base, run to a spot that is a few feet behind the point of the ball's descent (left). As the ball falls, run forward and catch it over your throwing shoulder (center). Take a crow hop, align your feet and shoulders to the target, and drop your arm down near your waist to maximize the distance and velocity of your throw (right).

the ball is hit in the air, quickly judge the point of its descent. Get to the spot immediately and take a few steps back from where the ball will land. As it falls, take two or three steps in, make the catch, and fire home. To make a strong throw, you have to take a few steps before releasing the ball, so why not take them as you're making the catch? It reduces your release time and gives you momentum.

Getting behind the ball is easy when a lazy fly ball is hit to your position. On balls hit deep to the outfield, however, turn your back to the ball and sprint. Once you've reached the area where you've predicted the ball will fall, turn your head to find the ball in the sky. Continue to glide back until you've gotten behind the ball, stop, and then take your steps back toward the infield to give you some momentum.

A common mistake outfielders make with this type of play is that they coast or drift back with the ball. As a result, they catch the ball moving away from the infield, or misjudge the length of the hit and miss the ball completely. Turn your back and run to your spot quickly. It's the most efficient method of making the play.

Catch the Ball Over Your Throwing Shoulder

One last tip when catching a fly ball and throwing when a runner is tagging up: catch the ball over your throwing shoulder. This position lets you catch the ball with your glove, transfer the ball into your throwing hand, drop your arm, and throw as quickly as possible. By catching the ball over your glove-side shoulder, you're forced to carry your glove laterally across your body, then grab the ball, drop your arm, and throw. The additional time allows the runner extra steps before you release the ball. It can mean the difference between a safe or out call.

Even when no runners are tagging up, catch the ball over your throwing shoulder. Make it a habit. Eventually, it will become one less item to think about.

Minimize Your Steps

In an effort to increase the velocity and strength of their throws, some outfielders take additional steps after catching the ball. This colossal error permits base runners to advance with little risk. Always remember: for every one step you take to throw the ball, the base runner gains two

When throwing to a cutoff man, aim for his chest.

strides. Although you may need an additional step or two to gain your balance, the increased time it takes to release the ball thwarts any chance of throwing out the runner. Have your momentum moving forward as you make the catch, take a crow hop, and fire to the base. An average throwing arm is greatly enhanced by a quick release.

GIVE THE INFIELDER A CHANCE

A strong throw and quick release are proficient only if the infielder is able to handle the ball. A throw that sails high or short-hops the receiver makes it difficult to receive the ball and apply a tag.

High throws offer the least chance of getting the runner. If the ball is thrown over the head of the receiver (out of reach), there is literally no chance of retiring the runner. If the receiver is forced to jump up or stretch his arm upward to make the catch, chances are slim. He's got to bring his glove back down to the ground, giving the runner time to slide underneath the tag. When throwing to a base, it's always better to bring the ball in low rather than high.

Short hops also present a problem for the receiver. It's difficult to cleanly catch a ball that lands a foot or two in front of you. The ground's surface or rotation of the ball makes it tough to predict how and where the ball will bounce. Even if the ball is caught cleanly, the receiver still needs recovery time to apply a tag.

If you can't reach the base in the air, aim your throw short enough so it reaches the receiver on a long bounce rather than a short hop. Long bounces are easier to handle, and the receiver will be able to set himself to make a quick tag once the ball arrives.

13

INFIELDER MAKING A PLAY ON A HIGH CHOPPER

The high chopper is a batted ball that approaches an infielder with one or more bounces whose apex is high overhead, perhaps 10 feet or more. It is usually moving slowly because the energy of the ball has been directed downward. The batter has struck the ball on part of its uppermost hemisphere, imparting topspin or forward spin, and sent it skyward toward the infield.

Study the Infield Conditions

Check all the areas of the infield, especially the area in front of home plate, which will influence the speed and height of ground ball bounces. Is it extra hard? Soft? Wet? Dry? Is the infield grass thick? Thin? Is the turf soft? Is the grass cut markedly low? Unusually high? Is the underlying turf hard? Are you on artificial turf? Study the bounces you get while taking batting practice and pregame ground balls. Prepare so you'll have a good idea of the bounces you will get even before the first pitch is thrown.

There are many reasons why a high chopper is a difficult play for an infielder, and why the ability to successfully make this play is considered an advanced or game-breaker baseball skill.

The ball's hang time is often significant enough to allow even a moderately fast runner to beat it out for an infield hit. The ball's trajectory may not allow a charging infielder to intercept it at a point where it is easy to snare the ball. The topspin may accelerate the ball as it strikes the ground again. The sun, at times, can interfere with the infielder's vision and ability to track the ball. The infielder may have too far to travel to reach the ball in time to make a play; this situation is more likely with a shortstop or second baseman making the play. Let's examine these troublesome characteristics.

1. *Significant hang time.* Because the ball does not come down for a few seconds (or more) the infielder must do everything he can to shorten the time. Most base runners can reach first base in four to five seconds, so there is little time for delay in getting to the batted ball. The infielder cannot hang back and wait for the ball to come to him. He must get on the move immediately. He then must make a judgment on the run as to exactly where the ball will be when he intercepts or reaches it.

    This is not always so easy. The easiest ground balls to catch are those that reach the infielder at the apex, what is often called a "Sunday hop," or at the very bottom of the arc, where the fielder can either "short-hop" or catch the ball as it reaches the ground. To short-hop a ball is to catch it just after it has hit the ground. The glove snags the ball just as it begins to rise again. First basemen deal with short hops all the time on low throws from the infielders. They reach out low with the glove and make a scooping, slightly rising movement toward the ball. The ball sticks in the pocket or webbing of the glove just inches off the ground.

    The most difficult play to make on a high chopper is when the infielder reaches the ball between a short hop and the apex—the "half-hop" position. Even major league players don't make this play as often as they'd like to. The difficulties are many, but the one that gives the most trouble is that you cannot always accurately judge where the ball will be in a half-hop. Because you are on the run and the ball is moving toward you, you have only a split second to judge the hop and move your glove hand or both hands to the right spot.

2. *Topspin.* When a high chopper is struck off an infield that is extremely hard it not only bounces high but also has extra forward spin. When it next bounces this topspin greatly accelerates the ball. This acceleration may alter the bounce by speeding it up, raising it a little higher than normal, or even angling it to one side slightly. Any of these small variations in the bounce will cause the ball to miss the fielder's glove pocket or webbing. Instead, it may just kick off the heel or side of the glove.

3. *The sun.* Especially later in the day, the sun can shine directly in the infielder's eyes as he raises his head to pick up the ball's trajectory or as he runs toward the ball to field it. To overcome the sun's blinding rays bring your glove up quickly above and in front of your head. Use your outstretched glove hand to shade your eyes. Keep moving forward and keep looking for the ball. It will suddenly drop down and out of the line between your eyes and the sun. Be ready to grab it.

4. *Too far to travel.* High choppers that are hit toward the middle infielders, the shortstop and second baseman, often don't allow enough time for the fielder to catch and throw the ball to first base in time to retire the runner. The difficulty of fielding these choppers is compounded by multiple hops. The infielder cannot wait to receive the ball. He must get moving even before he is certain at which point—that is, which high hop (after the first? second?), at which part of the arc of the hop—he'll be attempting to field it.

Here are some basic rules of thumb on how to make this play. But keep in mind, the high chopper is often a "do or die" play and there's no shame in missing now and then. In fact, when you've made the play you've mastered one of the most difficult game-breaker plays in baseball.

Determining How to Make the Play

1. The first thing is to start forward. Get on the move. It's a rare high chopper that allows you to stand your ground and wait for the ball to descend. A third baseman, first baseman, pitcher, or middle infielder playing close to the batter occasionally makes this play without charging—but usually the ball does not have extended hang time.

2. Determine whether you will be attempting the play when the ball is in short hop, half-hop, on the ground, or in the apex position.

3. If it is a short-hop situation, get your body to one side of the ball. You can try to scoop on the glove side and then throw or you can scoop and throw on the throwing side—both can work. Just remember to get rid of the ball on the very next step—you rarely have time for additional steps before throwing to first base.

As the pitcher releases each pitch, move inward to keep yourself on the balls of your feet. Remember, play the ball, don't let it play you.

Running in to field the ball before it can hit the ground is the easiest fielding play and affords you the most time to throw out the runner.

4. Because you are moving quickly through the ball as you field it and because the release of your throw is across your body, the flight of the ball will have a slight tailing motion to the right. And because you are making this throw while on the move your momentum will take you farther forward—and thus to the right of your target—as you release the ball. So start the ball to the left of your target, the first baseman. This will keep you from throwing the ball into the runner, especially if you are making the play from the third base position.

5. Quick footwork is important. As a general rule of thumb, if you are making a throw while on the move, that is, you do not have time to catch the ball, set your feet under you for a step, and throw, you should get your throw away with no more than two quick steps. For

Fielding the ball on the in-between hop is the most difficult play. If it's to your right, field it with a backhand. It's the most efficient method of catching the ball cleanly and being in a position to make a strong throw.

If you're forced to field the ball deep at the top of a bounce, plant your weight on your rear leg as you catch the ball, take a short directional step with your left foot, and fire immediately to first. If you catch the ball and then shuffle, you may not get the runner at first base.

example, if you catch the ball while your weight is on the right foot, take one more step—simultaneously gathering and gripping the ball and sighting the target with that first step—and then release the ball when your right foot next hits the ground again.

DRILL

Use batting practice. Assume your infield position and practice getting on the move whenever a topped ball of any kind is sent toward the infield. You want to build the habit of always closing toward a topped ball.

Have a coach or teammate purposely chop balls into the ground in sets of 10. Charge them; make the hand, glove, or body adjustments while on the move; and finish the play. Grade yourself. See if you can make the play 6 of 10 times without a fielding or throwing error. Then raise the goal to 7, 8, 9, and finally 10 of 10. Get used to making all of the quick judgments and varied plays that are necessary for mastering this play in its entirety.

14

FIRST BASEMAN CATCHING HALF-HOPS AND SHORT HOPS

At the major league level the position of first baseman often attracts converted third basemen, catchers, and outfielders, such as major leaguer Todd Zeile, a catcher and third baseman who also successfully mastered first base later in his career. Players who are converted to first basemen may have lost a little of their quickness, or they may play there to prolong their careers. Catchers who convert certainly can look forward to more injury-free play. Players who convert early in their careers from catcher to first base, such as the Brooklyn Dodgers' Gil Hodges, often are asked to make the change because they have the skills and body build that are best suited for first base play. Soft hands, good eye-hand coordination, and above-average height are a few of the prized characteristics. New York Met Mike Piazza, an extraordinarily gifted athlete, is a prime example of a catcher who could play first base before his career is over.

The most important skill of a first baseman is the ability to catch all kinds of batted and thrown balls. Without a clean catch of the ball at first base there can be no recorded out. Two of the most difficult catches that a first baseman must make are throws that reach him as half-hops and short hops.

Half-Hop Throws

A half-hop throw, which is more difficult than the short-hop throw, arrives low (in the dirt) and short of the player. The ball hits the ground or turf

When receiving a half-hop at first base, pull your glove-hand in toward your midsection as the throw arrives. Keep your body in front of the ball and use your throwing hand to cover and secure the ball.

several feet in front of the player and reaches the player at the approximate midpoint of the arc of its first bounce. The first baseman can neither scoop it—as a short hop—nor catch it at the apex, or very top of the bounce. He must find another way to catch it!

So how would you play a half-hop? On most infield plays and in most game situations, the first baseman doesn't try to simply block the ball, that is, drop to his knees and let it bounce off his body. This option would keep the ball in the infield and prevent any other runners from moving along. But it immediately eliminates the chance of retiring the runner at first base. So blocking a low throw at first base is rarely attempted. Rather, the first baseman attempts to catch the ball. In many cases, if he applies the correct technique, the first baseman can simultaneously try to make the catch and block the ball.

Making the Catch

Proper execution starts with getting to the bag early and determining which foot will contact the base and which foot will step toward the throw. For right-handed first basemen, on balls that are thrown to the left or center of the body, step with the left foot and place the right foot on the bag. For balls received slightly to the right, step with the left foot and backhand the ball. For balls thrown to the extreme right side, step with the right foot and place the left foot on the bag. You will avoid having to cross your left foot over the right foot when stepping and help keep proper balance. This split-second decision is made as the throw is released and the ball's flight is first sighted.

For left-handed first basemen, the footwork is somewhat easier. Step with the right foot, which is the same side as your glove hand, regardless of which side of your body the throw is made to.

1. Face your body directly at the player who is making the throw. Step toward the throw and keep your eyes focused on the throw. You'll know immediately when a throw is not going to reach you in the air. As soon as you've determined that the throw will be short in the dirt, make a judgment as to whether you can catch it on a short hop, full hop, or half-hop.

2. For a half-hop throw, stretch out and keep the ball in front of you, on either side of your knee. Drop the glove slightly below the level of the knee, fingers pointed down. Remember that you're expecting the ball to reach you at the midpoint of its bounce, not at the bottom or the top. If you anticipated the ball to be at the bottom, you would bring the glove down all the way to the ground. If it were going to bounce and reach you at the top of its arc you would keep the glove above the knee.

3. Bring your bare hand toward the glove. As the ball bounces, judge the midpoint height as best you can and bring the glove-hand up in a cradling motion, that is, pull it back and up toward you but keep the angle created at the elbow. Bring the bare hand over to help.

The bare hand will be especially helpful on throws that are received at the center of the body, to the inside of the knee. These are more difficult to judge and catch and the extra hand can sometimes close down on a ball that is still slightly loose in the webbing or pocket of the glove.

The ball, as it bounces, doesn't always rise to the precise level you've predicted, and the position of your body can help to keep the ball in front of you. You won't get the out at first base, but you will prevent the runner from taking an extra base. On balls received to the outside of the knee, the shoulder, arm, and left side of the chest will help you block the ball if you do not catch it cleanly. On balls to the inside of the knee your chest and abdomen will block the ball.

Short-Hop Play

On short-hop bounces, get into position for the throw but drop the glove low to the ground (at least to the level of the ankle) and make a scooping motion directly through the ball with the glove. Keep the glove open and move it forward aggressively. Try to take the ball at its shortest hop and snag it in the webbing or pocket. If you allow the ball to hit the heel of your glove you won't make a clean catch. On some throws that arrive closer to the center of the body, you can use the bare hand to help. However, this play is made more often with the glove-hand only.

Reach out for a short hop and look it into your glove. Scoop the ball upward as you catch it and show the umpire you caught it cleanly.

KNOW THE THROWS OF YOUR INFIELDERS

Each infielder delivers his throw with unique spin, carry, or arc. Keep their tendencies in mind when making adjustments to receiving their throws. Here are a few pointers:

- If the throw is across the diamond and released from a three-quarter position, allow for the ball to tail slightly toward home plate. When it bounces it will also bounce lower and to the home plate side.
- If the throw is more overhand, it will have a lot more backspin and carry, and the hop will be higher and straighter.
- If it's a sidearm throw, both the tailing action and bounce will be toward home plate.
- If the skin part of the infield is soft and pockmarked, the bounce will not be true. The ball will skid or bounce much lower than expected. Allow for a lower bounce by dropping the glove slightly. If the ball hits an uneven part of the dirt it will bounce lower and off-line. In this case, lower your entire body to block the ball should you fail to catch it.

15

FIRST BASEMAN MAKING A 3-6-3 DOUBLE PLAY ON A BALL CAUGHT ON THE INFIELD GRASS

The 3-6-3 double play is one of the prettiest plays executed on the baseball field. With a runner on first base and less than two outs, the first baseman fields a ground ball, throws it to second for the force-out, runs back to first base, and catches the throw from the shortstop to complete the double play. It involves quick hands and feet, accurate throws, and allows no margin for error. When performed properly, the 3-6-3 double play runs like a well-oiled machine with military-like execution.

The key to the 3-6-3 DP is quick and correct decision making by the first baseman. He's got to be in the right position to field the ball and must make an immediate decision. Is there a good opportunity to turn a double play, or is it safer to get the sure out at first base? A double play is the most desirable outcome, but not at the risk of getting neither out at first or second base. If the ball is hit slowly or to an area that makes it a gamble to go for the force-out at second, get the out at first base. When fielding a ground ball with runners on base, always make sure you get at least one out.

When to Go for the Double Play

Attempting to turn a double play is not automatic when the ball is hit to you at first base. It depends on where the ball is hit and how hard it is hit to you—a big reason why the 3-6-3 double play is highly difficult.

On crisply hit balls at you or to your right, go for the double play. A ball hit directly at you arrives very quickly, which allows you to field the ball and throw it to second base before the base runners can gain significant ground. When a ball is hit to your right, you're fielding the ball closer to second base, which shortens your throw. Also, your momentum, which is taking you toward second base, makes it easy to get some pop on your throw.

If the ball is hit to your left, take the sure out at first—unless the ball is hit extremely hard. In this case, you may still have a chance at the double play. In most cases, however, there isn't enough time to get both runners. Fielding the ball to your left takes you farther away from second base and shifts your momentum in the opposite direction. Avoid a potentially disastrous overthrow into left field and take the sure out at first base.

This also holds true on slow-hit balls and high choppers. If you have to move in for the ball or wait for it to come down before securing it in your glove, time will not permit you to turn the double play. Get the out at first base.

Getting into Position

With a runner on first base and less than two outs, you'll be holding the base runner on the bag. As the pitcher lifts his leg toward home plate, run a few steps in and to your right. More balls are hit between the first and second base hole than down the first-base line. In order to have a shot at turning the double play, you've got to field the ball as quickly as possible and make an accurate throw to second. It will be easier to do so if you've already moved in and to the right.

After hopping off of first base, get into a fielder's position. Stand on or at the edge of the infield grass. Spread your feet slightly farther than shoulder-width apart, and stand with your weight on the balls of your feet. Flex your knees and bend at the waist. Extend your glove hand out in front of you so it hovers just above the ground.

Turning the 3-6-3 Twin Killing

By fielding the ball on the infield grass, you'll have a clear path to throw the ball to the second base bag. Throw the ball to the infield side of second base. That way, the runner is not an obstruction. The shortstop will

Hold the runner on first base until you see the pitcher is going to home plate. Jump off the base and shuffle to your right in the fielder's position.

set up on the inside of second base and present a target with his glove. Whether you're a right-handed or left-handed first baseman, set your feet parallel to the throwing lane. If you're left-handed, take a short step or hop to square your feet and shoulders to the target. If you're right-handed, drop your right foot back and turn your body so it faces the outfield. Square your feet and shoulders to the target and throw. This maneuver can also be accomplished by a quick jump-spin to your right. Your feet trade places and your body goes from facing home plate to facing the outfield in an instant.

Using an infielder's release, throw the ball to the shortstop's chest so he's able to easily catch the ball and return a throw to first base. Do not drop your arm down to throw, which eats up too much time. Draw your arm straight back and fire a crisp, accurate throw.

The shortstop may not arrive at the base in time for an immediate throw. In this case, wait an instant and then lead him to the bag. In other words, throw the ball as if he were standing on the inside of the base.

Field the ball cleanly, align your feet and shoulders to second base, and throw the ball to the shortstop covering. Keep your throw to the left-field side of second base, so the shortstop can easily catch and throw to first base for the double play.

Make Sure of the First Out

Throw the ball first! Do not rush your throw or cut your follow-through short in an effort to hurriedly retreat to the first base bag. The lead runner is the most important out, and a poor throw will likely result in base runners being safe all around, possibly even advancing to the next base.

Once you've thrown the ball, immediately turn in toward the base. Sprint to the bag, and as you find the base with your foot, turn your body to second base. The ball may already be in flight, so it's important to get to the base as quickly as possible. If you're a left-hander, find the base with your left foot. Right-handers find the base with your right foot. Locate the ball and step toward the location it's thrown.

A common mistake made by first basemen is that they look for the ball before finding the base. You've got to find the base first. Catching the ball is useless unless your foot is on first base. Advanced players are able to cheat and look for the ball a little sooner because they've developed a feel for where first base is located. This is learned through years of playing experience.

Keys to Turning the 3-6-3 Double Play

- Shuffle off first base and into the fielder's position as the pitch is delivered.
- Make sure that the ball is hit hard enough at you or to your right to turn two.
- Field the ball cleanly and set your feet and shoulders parallel to second base.
- Make a crisp throw (chest-high) to the inside of the second base bag.
- Get back to first base quickly, turn to second base, and find the ball.

Common Mistakes When Turning the 3-6-3 Double Play

- Too slow off first base and failing to get into the fielder's position
- Making an ill-advised throw to second base when you've little chance of turning two
- Failing to get your feet underneath you before making the throw
- Rushing your throw or cutting it short to hurriedly run back to first base
- Failing to find first base before finding the throw from second base

Double plays can quickly smother an offensive rally. The 3-6-3 DP can really take the wind out of an opponent's sails and shift the momentum of a game. Practice this play each day to build confidence in your ability to execute without hesitation. The 3-6-3 double play is no easy task in the game, but when you pull it off, it's a work of art.

16

SECOND BASEMAN MAKING A DOUBLE-PLAY THROW TO SHORTSTOP ON A BALL HIT TO HIS LEFT

Second basemen rarely receive the notoriety that shortstops do in the infield. Shortstop is the glamour position, whereas second base seems more utilitarian. Both middle infield positions, however, are integral components to turning double plays. (And double plays are a pitcher's best friend.)

To enable the shortstop to make a quick turn and fire the ball to first base for the second out, the second baseman must give him a good feed. On balls hit to the second baseman's left side, the entire play relies on the quickness and accuracy of the second base feed.

This particular double-play turn speaks to balls hit at you that freeze you, or take you a few steps to your left. You are not able to underhand-toss or flip the ball to the shortstop in this situation. You've got to make a throw.

Getting into Position

Delivering the ball accurately and in time to the shortstop begins with your positioning. With a runner on first base and less than two outs, move a few steps in and over toward second base. Moving in allows you to field the ball sooner and moving over toward second base shortens your throw.

Take notice of the catcher's signal to the pitcher. Is it a fastball or off-speed pitch? If it's a fastball, stay in your customary double-play position. If the catcher calls for an off-speed pitch to a right-handed batter, cheat another step or two over toward second base. Off-speed pitches are predominantly pulled, so use this information to your advantage. Don't move, however, until the pitcher starts his delivery. Moving prematurely may tip off an observant hitter what type of pitch is coming.

On off-speed pitches to left-handers, cheat one step (at the most) to your left. Don't move too far, because you'll surrender too much ground up the middle. The defensive strategy is to be in position to turn a double play. You've got to give a little to get a little.

On balls hit directly at you, pivot your feet toward second base, dip your left knee, and send a crisp throw to the shortstop covering.

Making the Throw

There are two types of throws for you to learn for this situation—one where you simply pivot your feet and throw and another where you shift your feet and throw. The pivot throw is used when the ball is hit right at you or slightly to your left. Basically, if you're able to get your body in front of the ball and stop any momentum moving to your left before fielding it, use the pivot throw.

After you field the ball, pivot your left foot inward toward second base. Do not stand up! It wastes precious time. Bend down with your left knee, and turn your body to face second base. Keep your upper body upright as you pull the ball from your glove. Bring the ball straight up and back behind your ear and make a firm throw to the shortstop's chest. Do not lean back to put more on the throw. Quickness is more important than velocity.

Your feet never leave their spot on the ground during the pivot throw. Your left foot initiates your rotation by pivoting inward. Your right foot opens slightly as your body turns toward second base. There is no shuffle or step when executing this throw. Simply get your body in front of the ball as quickly as possible to field it, pivot, and make a short throw to second base.

Shifting Your Feet to Make the Throw

On plays where your weight is leaning toward first base as you field the ball, shift your feet to turn your body and throw. With your weight on your left leg, replace your feet. Move your right foot to the position held by your left and shift your left foot to the spot once held by the right foot. In one quick jump, your body turns 180 degrees to the right.

Shifting your feet is a quick, basic movement that puts you in a position to throw to second base. After fielding the ball, swing your right foot back and to the right, bringing your left foot forward toward second base. Your upper body turns to the right and your chest now faces the left-center field area. When the left foot plants, draw your arm back near your ear and fire a throw to your shortstop's chest.

Do not turn your body to the left and turn your back to the infield. First, it takes too much time. Second, your eyes lose sight of the infield and have to quickly pick the target up as you make the throw, leading to inaccurate throws.

On balls hit to your left, shift your feet so you're square to second base. A quick release is key to turning the double play on balls to your left.

THE UNDERHAND TOSS OR FLIP

The underhand toss or flip is used when balls are hit to your right, which takes you closer to the second base bag and makes an overhand throw unnecessary. Which technique you use usually depends on how hard the ball is hit and how quickly the shortstop arrives at second base.

On balls hit very hard, you've got some extra time to make the play. There is no need to rush. In addition, the shortstop will not be at the base prior to you receiving the ball. In this case, pivot inward toward second base and underhand-toss the ball to the shortstop. Toss the ball on a line so that it doesn't rise above the shortstop's chest.

On slow-hit balls to your right, the shortstop will be at or near the base as you field the ball. Time is of the essence, and you've got to get the ball to him quickly. Once you field the ball with two hands, shift your weight onto your right leg and flip the ball to the shortstop. With the ball in hand, extend your right hand outward and release the ball so it travels on a line to your target. Keep your body low to the ground for this throw. Standing up wastes time and makes a flip throw difficult to execute.

On balls hit slightly to your right, use a backhand flip throw to start the double play.
If the ball takes you far to your right, underhand-toss the ball to second base.

17

SECOND BASEMAN MAKING A DOUBLE PLAY WHEN RUNNER IS MAKING SLIDING CONTACT

Double-play turns appear to be routine when watching major leaguers play. Watching All-Stars Roberto Alomar and Omar Vizquel may give a false sense of reality. Alomar and Vizquel are among the very best in the world at their positions, and have taken thousands upon thousands of repetitions to make that play appear routine. Realistically, turning double plays is very hard and requires a significant amount of practice.

A Tough Routine

The double-play turn from the second base position is a tougher play than it is for the shortstop. Basically, you're running away from first base to receive the throw and catching the ball with your eyes facing the shortstop or third base area. These two elements make this play difficult because 1) you've got to stop your momentum from running in one direction, plant, and then throw in another direction; and 2) you're unable to see the base runner sliding into the base as you're catching the ball. These two factors, in addition to having to catch the ball and quickly release a strong, accurate throw to first base while avoiding an incoming runner sliding into your legs, make the double-play turn for the second baseman a tough play.

Getting into Position

Your positioning at second base is extremely important to making this play. With a force play at second base and less than two outs, move a few steps in and over toward second base. This position shortens the distance between you and second base and allows you to get to the base with enough time to get under control and make the turn.

Ultimately, you want to arrive at second base before or as the shortstop or third baseman catches the ground ball. This gives you ample time to brake down, set your feet, and decide which double-play turn method you will use. If you get to the base at or near the time the throw gets to the base, you'll be moving toward the ball too forcefully and will be unable to stop your momentum. In other words, you'll fly across the bag and have to make a very difficult throw across your body to first base.

As the ball is hit, sprint to the back of the base—the corner that points out to center field—and brake down your steps (take shorter, quicker steps) as you approach the bag. Set your shoulders parallel to first base as best you can. Hold your hands outward and chest-high to present a target. It's important to hold your hands out away from you 1) to catch the ball sooner, and 2) to transfer the ball from glove to hand as you pull your hands back inward to make the throw.

Sprint to the base on double-play ground balls. Get there as quickly as possible so that you have enough time to get your body under control and set your feet.

Bring your hands inward and circle them slightly down and to the right in one motion. In that one motion, you should receive the ball, bring it toward you while grabbing the ball with your throwing hand, pivot toward first base, and throw the ball. It has to be done in one continuous motion or the batter will reach first base safely.

The Double-Play Pivot

There are two important things to remember when turning a double play from second base. The first is to receive the ball and throw to first as quickly as possible. The second is that there is a runner sliding into second base attempting to knock your legs out and alter or stop your throw. You have to move away from second base to get out of harm's way.

The runner is bound by the rules to slide directly into second base. The areas to the right, left, and behind second base are safety areas from which you can make your throw. Choose one of the areas to throw from and move to that spot as you receive the feed. Your choice of location is based on two factors: where the ball is hit and your personal level of comfort. Each player has his own preference as to which pivot play works best. Read each pivot below and determine which works best for you.

THE HURDLER'S HOP

The hurdler's hop is used by middle infielders when turning double plays. It's a technique used to avoid contact by base runners attempting to slide into their legs. Here is how it works.

When you release the ball, your weight is shifted onto your left leg. After you release the ball and complete your follow-through, your upper body shifts forward. Using your left leg to push off, lift your right leg straight up by bending at the knee. Jump up into the air and raise your left leg into the air by bending at the knee. As your left leg reaches its peak, your right leg falls to the ground and keeps your balance. This quick hop, as if over a hurdle, lifts your feet up and out of the way for just enough time to avoid the sliding base runner.

Stepping Across the Base

On balls hit to the third baseman or to the right of the shortstop, place your left foot on the third-base-side edge of second base. Rest your heel

On balls hit to third base or to the shortstop's right, step on top of the base with your left foot (left). Once you see the ball is thrown accurately, step across the bag with your right foot. Catch the ball as you plant with your right foot, step with your left foot and throw to first base (right).

on the base and your toes on the ground. Stand on the right-hand side of the base. As the ball is thrown, step to the ball with your right foot by pushing off with your left foot. Time this motion so that your right foot plants as you catch the ball. Your right foot should plant approximately two to three feet past the base.

Don't step to the ball until you identify the throw. Stepping prematurely hinders your ability to catch the ball cleanly if the throw is wild. See the ball first, and then step to it.

As the right foot plants, your left foot leaves the base, moves forward briefly to square up with the right foot, and then steps toward the first baseman. Throw the ball crisply to first base and then hop over the sliding runner to complete the double play. Stepping across the bag with your right foot takes you out of the path of the runner.

Using the Base as Your Shield
On balls to the left of the shortstop or on balls that move him back to his left, place your left foot along the left-field-side edge of the base. This foot

On a ball that takes the shortstop back and to his left, put your left foot on the back of the base (left). Receive the throw, rock back on your right leg, and transfer your weight forward as you throw to first base (right). Use the base to protect you from the runner.

position puts the second base bag between you and the runner. Shift your weight onto your right leg and hold your glove out with two hands at chest level.

As you catch and transfer the ball into your throwing hand in one motion, draw your arm back and transfer your weight forward. Your left foot remains pressed against the side of the base. Fire the ball to first base and crow hop. The bag is there to protect you, but a base runner may slide in high and come over the base.

Stay Behind the Base

Sprint to the back of the base. Put your left foot against the back of the base and await the throw. If the throw is on target, push back off the base with your left foot and shift your weight onto your right leg. Catch the ball with two hands, circle up to the throwing position, step to first base, and fire an accurate throw.

Pushing off of second base takes you out of the path of the runner. It's important that you stop your momentum from moving backward before

Step on the base with your left foot and extend your glove to receive the throw (left). As the ball reaches the base, step back off the base with your left foot, catch the ball as you plant on your right foot, step with your left foot and throw to first base (right).

throwing the ball. If you're falling back, errant throws can flare up. Accept the weight with your right leg, and then transfer your body weight toward first base upon release. Hop over an aggressive runner.

Cheating Is Allowed

On double-play turns, umpires often will allow you to leave the bag slightly before catching the ball, come across it without touching it, or even step to the side or back off of the base prior to receiving the ball. They make this allowance to protect you. Injuries can occur if you stand in harm's way for too long, so umpires are known to let you leave a little early.

With two outs, umpires will not be so forgiving. Because you're not turning a double play and there is no danger, they will require you to stay on the base. Treat the play like you're a first baseman and hold the bag.

THE MAZ

Pittsburgh Pirate second baseman Bill Mazeroski played in six all-star games during his Hall of Fame career. Although his most memorable moment was hitting a game-winning home run in the seventh game of the 1960 World Series against the Yankees, his distinction is being known as the greatest fielding second baseman in the history of baseball.

At his first all-star appearance in 1958, players on both the National and American League teams stopped to watch Mazeroski take infield practice. They gazed on his artistry of the double-play turn—a lightning-fast side step and swift throw to first—with the same respect that they watched Ted Williams take batting practice. He earned the nickname "No Touch." The ball arrived and departed from second base so quickly that it seemed as if Mazeroski never touched the ball. He simply redirected it to first base.

Accomplished major league players watched Mazeroski in awe, which tells you that turning the double play from second base entails more than rudimentary skills. It takes positioning, body coordination, instinct, and most importantly quickness. Maz took pride in mastering the art of "turning two" and solidified a home in Cooperstown, New York, as a result.

18

SHORTSTOP MAKING A PLAY FROM THE THIRD BASE–SHORTSTOP HOLE

Derek Jeter, Omar Vizquel, Nomar Garciaparra, Alex Rodriguez. We've seen them all commit this act of thievery. A batter rips a ball to the left of the third baseman, and assumes he's got himself a base knock. Suddenly, the shortstop appears on the radar screen. He fields the ball with his backhand, and with supernatural quickness, uncorks a long, powerful throw toward first base. The first baseman strides forward with his lead leg, extends his glove-arm outward, and engulfs the ball into his mitt an instant before the batter's outstretched foot reaches the first base bag. The umpire takes one step toward the play and then throws a right cross to punch the runner, "Out!" The runner looks to the sky in utter bewilderment, questioning how something he rightfully earned was taken from him in a matter of seconds.

Each of the players mentioned attacks this play differently. To teach you, for example, Jeter's technique of backhanding the ball on the run, taking another step toward the outfield, then leaping up, turning, and throwing the ball in midair is a little too much to ask. With all due respect, there is a reason why Jeter plays shortstop for a team in New York that has won four world championships since 1996. He possesses innate skills unmatched by 99.9 percent of the people who wear a baseball uniform. Instead of assuming you wear pinstripes, we'll describe the most efficient method of executing this play, which is among the most difficult in baseball.

Your first step is critical when fielding balls hit to your right. Cross over with your left foot to turn your body sideways so you can run laterally to the ball.

The Immediate Crossover Step

Your first step is extremely significant to gloving a ball in the shortstop hole. As soon as you see the ball is hit to your right, cross your left foot over your right foot and turn your body sideways to the ball. This crossover step must be immediate. Any hesitation or stutter-step eliminates your chances of throwing the runner out at first.

After taking your crossover step and turning your body sideways, run directly to the spot at which you'll intercept the ball. The precise location of that spot is determined by the speed of the batted ball and how far to the right of you it's hit. Your intent is to field the ball with your backhand without diving, which may force you to angle your run back and to the right. By running directly to your right and not angling back, you may have to dive for the ball in order to stop it from getting through the infield.

The Final Crossover Step

Stopping and starting quickly are essential to infield play. Starting swiftly increases your range, while stopping quickly allows you to get your body under control to make plays consistently. As you approach your target area

If time permits, reach across your body with your backhand and field the ball off your left foot. Look the ball into the glove; don't peek at the runner.

and the ball arrives, brake down your steps. Time your final steps so that your left foot crosses over your right on your last step. This position will allow you to backhand the ball. Your left foot and left hand are closest to the ball when you catch it. This footwork is critical, as it gives you the longest reach with your backhand and also positions your feet for the final stage—the plant and throw.

As your left foot crosses over for your final step, bend at the waist and knees and shift your weight onto your left leg. Lower your body and eyes to the ball. Reach over with your left arm and turn your glove-hand over (clockwise) so the fingers point to the ground. Hold the glove slightly to the right of your left foot, an inch or so above the infield dirt. With your weight leaning heavily on your left leg, follow the ball (with your eyes) into your glove.

As you field the ball, take one more step with your right foot. Plant on your right foot and shift your weight back. Turn your head to face the target, square your shoulders, take a short directional step with your lead foot, and fire an overhand throw to first base. The throw is from deep in the hole, so there is little time. Only a strong throw will arrive at the base in time to get the runner.

An important factor in making this play is getting to the spot with enough time to set your feet. You've got to select an area that you can get

Step to the right with your right foot and plant it to stop your momentum from moving away from first base. Take a short directional step toward first base with your left foot and transfer your weight forward to make a strong throw.

to before the ball arrives. If you and the ball reach the spot simultaneously and you're running hard when you make your final step, your momentum will continue away from first base. Unable to control your body, you'll be forced to attempt a throw from an unbalanced position moving away from the target. The strength of your throw diminishes, as will your level of accuracy. Get to the spot early enough so that you can brake down and control your momentum before making that final crossover step.

PUSH SIDEARM THROWS TO THE SIDE

Major league players are notorious for fielding routine ground balls and flipping a sidearm toss to first base. They make everything look very easy; hence the term "routine." Avoid getting into this habit. It is not the most efficient way to throw the baseball and can lead to unwarranted "safe" calls at first base. Throw the ball overhand to maximize speed, accuracy, and backspin carry.

Major league players can get away with throwing the ball sidearm (on routine plays) for numerous reasons. Batted balls by major league hitters are struck harder than amateur league players, and the ball gets from point A to point B more swiftly. Low-cut grass and perfectly manicured infields also contribute to the speed of ground balls. Big league infielders also correctly charge balls. They don't wait back on their heels for the ball to get to them. Charging the ball shortens the distance and reduces the time it takes to receive the ball. Infielders at the major league level have the ball in their hands much faster than high school or collegiate level players. As a result, they can flip the ball sidearm to first base. In addition, major league players are grown men who possess superior arm strength. A sidearm flip from them may travel at the same speed as when you uncork an overhand throw.

Your strongest, straightest throws are made when the ball is released overhand. Don't get lazy and drop your arm down. Stay on top of the ball when you throw.

19

SHORTSTOP MAKING A DOUBLE PLAY WHEN RUNNER IS MAKING SLIDING CONTACT

It's easy to understand the truth in the baseball axiom, "The double play is the pitcher's best friend." One pitch results in two outs. But execution of the play is not always easy. For one, the runner leaving first base tries to break up the double play (see "30. Breaking Up a Double Play"). By successfully disrupting the infielder covering second base he will keep the rally alive. Middle infielders—the shortstop and second baseman—have to learn how to deal with contact from the oncoming runner and still complete the throw to first base to record the second out.

Gauging the Speed of the Hit

The speed at which a potential ground ball reaches one of the infielders affects the way a shortstop makes the play. For example, sharply hit ground balls provide more time for the throw to second base, and generally more time for the shortstop to tag second base and make the throw to first base. But on this play he often has to throw over or around or directly toward an oncoming runner who has not yet reached the base, and many times, not cleared the throwing lane by sliding. On this play, the shortstop must throw the ball directly at the first baseman and trust that the runner will at the very last moment run to the side or slide in the base path several feet short of the base. If there is adequate time, the shortstop can also step to the side, away from the path of the oncoming runner, to a spot that opens a clear throwing lane to first base and then throw the ball.

In all, shortstops can employ several techniques and methods to make the double play. Here are the most common ways.

1. *When the shortstop has lots of time to receive the ball and make the throw.* This situation is usually the result of a hard-hit or moderately fast ground ball reaching the infield. Move quickly to an area just behind the back of the base, perhaps two to three feet, and prepare to receive the ball. Here's a way to test for the correct position: reach your arms to full length and your hands should be over the base. By staying slightly behind the base you leave all options open to you, especially an allowance to adjust for errant throws. If you go all the way to the base, that is, straddle it, or set up in front of the base, you cannot catch a throw that is behind you and recover. Your momentum (as you reach back toward the outfield) takes you away from the base and away from first base, the direction of your intended throw. So stay slightly behind the base to keep every play in front of you, and preserve the possibility of recovering from a bad throw and still completing the double play.

When turning the double play from shortstop, run to the back of second base (left). As you receive the throw from the second baseman, swipe the back of the base with your right foot as you shift your feet to the left to make the throw.

If the runner is not close to the bag, that is, has not begun to slide, take the throw and simultaneously drag your back foot across the back of the base. Next, step to the right-field side of second base with your left foot and make a clean, unimpeded throw to first base. If the throw brings you to the inside part of second base, that is, toward the pitcher's mound, simply shuffle to the right, stepping on second base with your left foot, then off the base to the right side to complete the throw. If the throw brings you directly over the base, jump on the base with the rear (or right) foot, place the left foot in front of the base, and make the throw. You will be in front of the base but able to move away before the sliding runner reaches you.

When you receive the ball with plenty of time to tag the bag and make the throw, the runner can often be in the way of the throw. Don't let him distract you. Pick up the first baseman and concentrate on a direct throw. Almost without fail, the runner will move out of the way, especially when he sees that you are throwing down the same lane in which he is running.

2. *When the shortstop and runner reach the base at the same time, or at nearly the same time.* Remember that the runner can slide into you at second base as long as he can touch the base with one of his hands. If the runner slides beyond, that is, to one side or the other to make contact with you, he and the runner attempting to reach first base will be called out. This is interference, a call determined by the umpire's judgment. One way to help diminish the effectiveness of a base runner's attempt to break up the double play is to stay behind the base throughout the play. Receive the ball behind the base, step onto the base with your left foot, rock back onto your right foot, and throw. This technique is usually effective if the runner arrives a split second after you've finished delivering the throw.

A Quick Jump

Another common way to avoid the runner is to jump over him—a timing play. Throw and leap. Or throw while leaping. The latter won't allow you to get as much velocity on the ball but it still might get to first base in time to double a slower runner. This play, which is the most athletic and most spectacular, needs practice and repetition. Refer to "The Hurdler's Hop" in "17. Second Baseman Making a Double Play When Runner Is Making Sliding Contact" to learn how to make this move.

DRILL

You will need a soccer ball, a basketball, and a beach ball. For the first phase of this drill, place the beach ball in front of second base, touching the side closest to first base. Approach the base and take the throw from the second base side. Time your approach so that when you receive the ball your weight is either slightly on the rear foot or evenly distributed. If you receive the ball with your weight slightly on your rear foot, step immediately on the edge or top of the base in combined tagging/throwing motion and deliver the ball. Then leap over the beach ball. If you receive the ball with your weight on your left foot or on both feet (for example, the ball is delivered to your left and you must shift onto your left foot to catch it), quickly shift the weight to the back foot (as in a quick crow hop), step with the left foot, and throw. In this play, tag the base either with the front foot when you step to throw or with the back foot by dragging the back foot across the back of the base. Then leap over the ball.

For the second phase, have someone roll the soccer ball toward the base, make the tag of second base, throw, and then time your leap over the oncoming ball. Repeat the same drill with the basketball and beach ball. This drill also can be done using a plastic garbage can. Simply place it along the first base side of second base and repeat the prescribed footwork to tag the base, make the throw, and leap over the can.

Aggressive base runners will slide into your feet to stop or alter your throw to first base. Take a hurdler's hop after you release the ball to protect yourself from injury.

20

THIRD BASEMAN MAKING A PLAY ON A SLOW ROLLER

The slow-rolling ground ball to third base is one of the most difficult plays in baseball because the grounder comes in disguise—a weak roller coming off a full swing, a gross miss-hit that can bring an unplanned base hit. The third baseman "reads" the powerful swing and momentarily freezes, expecting a hard-hit ball, only to realize in the next split second that the ball is rolling slowly toward him instead. Momentarily frozen, he must now come forward as quickly as possible, make a quick decision to field the ball either bare-handed or with the glove and bare hand, and maintain his balance while bending low and whipping a laser throw across his body to first base.

Deep Trouble

Often on this play the third baseman is playing farther back, that is, in an area closer to the back cut of the infield. There is a lot of infield ground to cover in the time it takes to make the play. The difficulty is compounded further by the angle at which the third baseman must make his approach to the ball and throw to first base. Running parallel to the third base foul line, the angle of the throw approaches 90 degrees, and it is made at full gallop. There is very little margin for error.

Charge the ball on a line so that you can field the ball to your left side.

As you field the ball with two hands, take one step to gather control of the ball.

1. The first rule of thumb is to get on the move immediately. You don't have time to figure out at which bounce you and the ball will meet. It may not be a bounce by the time you get there—the ball may be rolling completely on the ground. So get moving!

2. If the ball is nearly slowed to a stop, try to pick it up with one hand. While moving quickly forward, place your throwing-side foot, the right foot, next to the ball, and then reach down with the right hand in a *backward sweep*. (Note: This play is also made with the palm up, fingers down when there still is a little hop to the ball as you reach it.) Open your hand wide and take the ball as quickly and efficiently as possible. Getting a perfect grasp is not always possible, so don't worry about it. The ball will rest mostly in your fingertips, as it is almost impossible to grip and cradle the ball in the palm while on a dead run. Take one more step with the left foot and throw the ball as the right foot hits the ground. You don't have time for any more steps.

Take one final step to release the ball off your right foot.

A quick release is essential, so stay slightly bent over and deliver a sidearm throw to first base.

In the brief time you are bringing the ball under control in your right hand, roll it as best you can into your fingertips. Make this throw with two, three, or four fingers wrapped around the ball. It doesn't matter. You can make a good throw regardless of the number of fingers holding the ball. With practice, you will be able to quickly slide your pinky and ring finger alongside the ball and form a normal two-fingered grip.

Focus on an area to the left of the first baseman as you aim and deliver the throw. If you don't, the natural tailing or rotation of the ball and your forward momentum will cause the ball to travel into the runner's path.

3. If the ball is still bouncing, anticipate and judge whether you will reach the ball at its apex, its lowest point, or somewhere in between. Catching and throwing a ball at the very top of its bounce, or apex, is the easiest play. If you make the play bare-handed, take the ball alongside (your body to the left of the ball), with your right foot on

the ground. Release the ball on the very next step (with the left foot). If you make this play with two hands, catch and throw with one complete, continuous motion.

If you reach the ball at its lowest point, make two steps after getting control of the ball—right foot to plant and left foot to deliver the throw.

If you reach the ball and must catch it on a short hop, approach the ball on your glove side and make the play one-handed with the glove. Drop the glove down and make a scooping motion, snagging the ball in the pocket or webbing. Take one step with the right foot as you transfer the ball to the throwing hand and then deliver the ball as your left foot hits the ground.

If you reach the ball in what's known as a half-hop or in-between hop, approach the ball with the center of your body slightly to the right of the ball's path. You can make this play with glove-hand only or with both hands, but keep your body behind the ball. Judge where the ball will be as you reach it, but if you misjudge slightly you can still make the play. You can trap the ball against you or you might tip it slightly in the air, catch it, and make the throw. Of all the plays, the slowly hit grounder that you reach at mid-hop, or half-hop, is the most difficult. But never give up. You will surprise yourself and your teammates if you're aggressive and decisive when confronted with this play.

DRILL

Place a half-dozen balls alongside the third-base line about two feet apart and halfway between third base and home plate. Practice running to the ball, grabbing the ball with a backward motion, and throwing across your body to first base. Repeat, but have someone roll the balls. Repeat again, but have your partner hit the balls with a fungo bat. Make sure the fungoed balls are varied, from high-hopping, slow grounders to slow, on-the-ground rollers. Your goal is to field 10 consecutive rollers cleanly before quitting.

Here is another drill to improve the across-the-body, sidearm throw that is necessary for this play. Move to a spot about 10 feet away from home plate along the first-base foul line. Stand 10 to 12 feet inside the line. Place a ball in your throwing hand, lean forward, and lower your body (as if you had just picked up a rolling grounder). Take four steps (in order to build some momentum to simulate game conditions), leading with the right foot and staying low, and deliver the ball to first base. Make the throw with a sidearm motion. Release the ball just as your throwing hand reaches the first-base foul line. Attempt to keep the ball in the fair territory of the infield. Properly thrown, the ball will tail slightly toward foul territory but reach first base in fair territory. Make the necessary adjustments. After mastering this skill along the first-base line, move to the third-base line, about 15 to 20 feet from home plate, and continue the drill. Your goal is 10 perfect consecutive throws from each side before you quit.

PITCHING

Introduction

During his rookie season in 1987, Greg Maddux compiled a 6–14 record with the Chicago Cubs. He gave up 181 hits in 155 innings and finished the season with an ERA of 5.61. Randy Johnson was 7–13 in his first full season in the major leagues. After going winless in his first four decisions with the Montreal Expos and surrendering 29 hits and 26 walks in 29 innings, he was traded to the Seattle Mariners. As a rookie in 1988, Curt Schilling was 0–3 in four starts with the Baltimore Orioles. His ERA was a lofty 9.82. Schilling was sent to the bullpen for the next two years before being traded to the Houston Astros. It wasn't until 1992 when he was acquired by the Philadelphia Phillies that he blossomed into a full-time starter.

All three of these pitchers were good enough to pitch in the major leagues in the late 1980s, yet they failed to produce satisfying results (by their standards). And today, all three of them are among the elite pitchers in baseball. They are the best of the best and own eight Cy Young awards and numerous strikeout crowns between the three of them.

What those early career numbers show is that even major league pitchers have room for improvement. Most veteran pitchers admit that when they were younger, they felt they knew what it took to get hitters out. They could get guys out with their arm. Today, they get hitters out with their head just as much as their arm. Good pitching is about attacking hitters with an approach, and then making adjustments along the way.

It Takes More Than Talent

Many young pitchers in amateur baseball leagues stumble upon pitches that have incredible life and movement. Breaking pitches are often referred to as "nasty" and pitches that tail or sink may be considered "wicked." But the question remains, can that nasty breaking pitch be thrown for a strike? Is that wicked sinker thrown with a purpose? Great stuff allows you to coast through the rudimentary levels of the game, but it takes more than a healthy pitching repertoire to get good hitters out.

Each hitter you face presents a one-on-one battle with a new enemy. Don't expect to get every hitter out the same way. They all have individual strengths to be cautious of, and individual weaknesses to attack. A high fastball might overmatch one hitter, but the next batter might hit that same pitch a country mile.

Detecting weaknesses in a hitter can be of great help, especially early in the game. It offers you a point of attack. That said, good hitters adjust each time they step up to the plate. If you've gotten a batter out a certain way, you can bet that he's aware of how he's been retired. Also, he's now seen you a few times. He's seen your pitches, knows your release point(s), and has gauged your speed. It's important to stay smart and live in the present, rather than the past. What worked for you before may not work again. Respect the damage that can be inflicted by the man holding a bat.

Pitching successfully takes more than having a good arm. It entails thought, working ahead of hitters, disrupting timing, getting them to swing at your pitch, holding runners close, fielding your position, adjusting your pitching plan, and competing harder than ever when you don't have your best stuff. Maddux, Johnson, and Schilling each had fresher arms in the formative years of their careers, but by learning how to pitch, they registered much higher winning percentages later on. Learn from their growing pains and start the improvement process today.

21

THROWING THE CURVEBALL FOR STRIKES

"One of the best fastballs I'd ever thrown was hit for a home run (by the Braves' Joe Torre). I learned the hard way that it would not be possible to get by in the major leagues with just a fastball, no matter how hard it was thrown."

—NOLAN RYAN

Whether you're in the major leagues or in high school, you need to develop a breaking ball to compete successfully. And you need to throw it consistently for strikes. At higher levels of baseball, if you can't throw curveballs for strikes hitters will simply take the curveball for a called ball and look for the pitch you can get over the plate. If you find yourself in this situation, the advantage swings dramatically to the hitters.

Also, at the higher levels of baseball you will encounter more players who can hit your fastball, so you'll need another pitch or two. In high school, you may throw fewer than 20 breaking balls in a 100-pitch game. Combined with a good change-up, you may throw even fewer. But you'll need a breaking ball to help you get the outs you need.

Creating Movement and a Change of Pace

The curveball is the most effective breaking ball to learn because it not only moves—changes direction, moving down and to the side—but it is also a change-of-pace pitch that can a throw off a hitter's timing. The three-quarter curveball, which is released from a two o'clock position and travels roughly to eight o'clock (in a 2–8 arc), is the easiest to learn, and less strenuous on the arm and shoulder muscles. The three-quarter curveball gives you both lateral and downward movement.

The two o'clock arm slot—a point of release that corresponds to the position of the number two on the face of a clock—is only an approximation. Your natural motion may release the ball slightly higher, that is, closer to one o'clock, which is more overhand, or slightly lower, that is, closer to three o'clock, which is sidearm. Be careful not to drop too far below two o'clock because you will have difficulty getting the ball to move downward.

Achieving Maximum Rotation

"Kids are anxious to throw curveballs, and the more you throw them the better you get. But with young players, it is dangerous to throw too many. At 13 or 14 years of age, a player can start throwing a limited number of curveballs, assuming he employs proper mechanics. Studies have shown that players' tendons, ligaments, and muscles at this age are not fully developed and there's a great likelihood you can cause injury with overuse. I think age 18 is a safer age to throw a curveball with regularity."

—GALEN CISCO

The four-seam curveball grip

The two-seam
curveball grip

A four-seam grip can be used to throw the curveball. Like the four-seam fastball, it allows you to get maximum rotation on the ball. To throw a four-seam curve, find one of the wide gaps between the seams and place your middle finger along the inside of the right seam (for a right-hander). Lay your index finger alongside your middle finger. Apply pressure with the middle finger along the seam. Place your thumb underneath the ball, slightly bent and on the seam. A line drawn from your middle finger to

Gripping a curveball with more of the pressure on your finger pads (as shown) produces a faster-breaking pitch with sharper break. Holding the ball farther back toward the palm of your hand produces a slower-breaking pitch with a more gradual break. The former allows more wrist snap and thus a faster rotation.

your thumb cuts the ball in half. Stabilize the ball with the inside of your ring finger with the joint closest to your fingertips resting on the seam across from your thumb.

You can vary the velocity and rotation of the curve by moving the ball either closer to your fingertips or back toward the palm. If you move the ball toward the fingertips, thus creating more space between the palm and ball, and press the ball against the second joint and fingertips, you can create a slower-spinning, slower-traveling, wider-breaking curveball. If you move the ball toward the palm and away from the fingertips, thus creating less space between the palm and ball, and press the ball against the entire length of the finger and part of the palm closest to the base of the fingers, you can create a faster curveball with a sharper but shorter break.

Curveball grips can—and should—be customized to your hand. Experiment with different grips to find out which works best for you and what modifications can bring movement and breaking action.

When throwing a breaking pitch, your throwing arm finishes across your midsection (as shown). When throwing a fastball, your arm finishes lower, near your knee.

Think Fastball

When you throw the curveball, your delivery is nearly identical to your fastball's. Your arm follows the same path as it does on your fastball, but as it passes your ear, turn your wrist so that the palm of your hand is facing the side of your head rather than toward home plate. Keep the wrist straight and relaxed.

After it passes by your ear, rotate the wrist forward and allow the ball to roll over the index finger and out toward the target. Push up with the thumb and keep the middle finger pressed against the seam until the ball releases.

Follow through with your elbow coming down along the outside of the knee of your stride leg.

Visualization

Visualization can help you master the curveball. You start a curveball at one position and expect it to move quite a distance downward and sideward to reach the target. Shouldn't you have a vision in your mind's eye as to how it will look as it moves toward the target? Yes, because it can focus your mind's eye on exactly what is intended, and it can give you the confidence to "throw the pitch" and not "aim it" or "steer it."

So, give yourself a good image of how the ball will travel on the way to the target. Imagine its speed, its trajectory, and its arrival at the waiting target. Use this image to help you make a free and relaxed motion. Remember, *focus on the target but imagine the arc, speed, and movement* down and to the side as the pitch is released.

22

THROWING CHANGE-UPS FOR STRIKES

"After you learn a fastball, you should learn how to throw a change-up. The reason a change-up is so effective is as simple as this: hitters recognize the fastball spin on a change-up, but they don't recognize the change in speed. This upsets their timing, and this is the essence of pitching. In addition, the change-up can be thrown more consistently for a strike than any other non-fastball pitch. Without question, the change-up is a powerful weapon in a pitcher's arsenal."

—JOE KERRIGAN

There is no better second pitch than the change-up. It will generate a lot of weak grounders or swinging strikes without taking much out of you. It does not strain your arm, it should be easier to throw for strikes than a breaking ball, and the stiffer your competition, the more important it is to have in your repertoire. It will make your fastball look faster, and it can be psychologically devastating to hitters.

The Circle Change

One of the more popular change-ups is the circle change. It gets its name by the circle the index finger and thumb form along the side of the ball. You can grip the ball at least two different ways. One way is to form the circle with the thumb and index finger meeting where the seams are closest (thumb and finger resting against the seam closer to the fingertips and

The circle
change-up
grip

front of the ball) and place the tips of the middle finger and ring finger across the seam. The pinky finger rests alongside the ball, opposite the circle. A line drawn through the ball between the pinky and the point where the tips of the thumb and index finger meet would bisect the ball. This grip gives a four-seam rotation.

Vary this grip by moving the thumb and index finger back a little, placing them on the seam closest to the palm. This will move the ball slightly off center and creates (for right-handed pitchers) a slight sideward/downward rotation that will fade the ball away from left-handed hitters and inside and down to right-handed hitters.

Another change-up grip that creates a fadeaway and downward arc is to grip the ball along the narrowed seams with the index and middle finger, thumb resting on the seam that runs on the left hemisphere. Move the ball toward the fingertips and keep pressure on the left side of the index finger. When releasing the ball press down with the index finger and give the ball screwball rotation, that is, counterclockwise. Keep up your arm speed and throw the ball with the same delivery as a fastball.

Whatever change-up grip you use, remember that it's the grip that takes the speed off the pitch. Throw it with the same arm speed as your regular fastball. Don't try to take anything off this pitch with anything other than the new grip. When playing catch practice throwing change-ups. You will gain a higher level of comfort with the grip, throwing motion, and natural action of your throws.

As you move to higher levels of competition concentrate on putting the pitch in the lower half and on the outer half of the strike zone. If you can add movement to the change of speed, so much the better, but a change in velocity and consistency in the strike zone will be enough to get hitters out.

Challenging the Hitter

Throwing a change-up does not make you a passive pitcher. Being aggressive as a pitcher does not mean throwing the ball as hard as you can or overpowering your opposition. It means throwing pitches in the strike zone and challenging the hitter to do something with them. Listen to what the Seattle Mariners' left-handed pitcher Jamie Moyer has to say about being aggressive. He has a change-up in the low 70s, a below-average fastball, and a winning major league record.

Moyer says, "I don't feel like I've ever gone out and dominated a league or a hitter. And I don't want ever to feel that way. Maybe if I threw 95 miles per hour I'd look at it differently. . . . If I have to go after hitters, I challenge them, but I challenge them by using different sides of the plate, different speeds, different looks."

You will find that you can use a change-up against just about every type of hitter you will face, with the exception of the batter who simply cannot catch up to your fastball. Never throw a change-up to the batter who is late on your fastball. It simply speeds up his bat.

Change-ups that are kept low and out of the strike zone plague hitters. They are difficult to take because they appear to be fastballs that are low strikes. They generally produce weakly hit balls or swings and misses.

Look for Long Striders

During batting practice or during a batter's first at-bat, notice whether the hitter takes a very long stride and thus has a difficult time keeping his weight back. These batters are typically very aggressive fastball hitters, and if they connect the ball can go a long way. But it is hard for these hitters to keep their weight back (and more importantly their hands back), so you can throw off their timing with a change-up. They will be way out in front of the pitch, swinging and missing, trying to hold up, or connecting weakly because all of their weight is on the front foot.

"Developing a change-up has been the biggest adjustment for me. It's a pitch that I have to throw if I'm going to successful. You've got to change speed more in the starting role because you're facing hitters three and sometimes four times throughout a game instead of seeing them once out of the bullpen."

—DARREN DREIFORT

Most long-striding hitters try to make contact with pitches out in front of the plate to pull the ball, but there are some short striders who try to pull everything as well. If you notice that a right-handed hitter won't try to take your outside pitches up the middle or to the right side, you've got an excellent candidate for a change-up over the outer half of the plate.

The path of a pull hitter's swing through the hitting zone leaves him only the end of the bat with which to hit the ball. If he's a pull hitter who "steps in the bucket"—steps away from the plate as he swings—he will be even more vulnerable to a change-up away.

23

HOLDING RUNNERS ON FIRST BASE

Few baseball skills can make or break a game for a pitcher more than that of holding runners on base. In lower-level youth league play, such as Little League competition, pitchers are not required to hold runners on base—leads are prohibited and the pitcher is free to concentrate on pitching to the batter. However, at higher levels of competition holding a runner on base is an important advanced skill that must be mastered if a pitcher is to compete successfully. For our discussion, we will focus on holding a runner on first base, which is encountered most often.

Understanding the Rules

Here is a brief review of the rules of thumb for pitching from the stretch. You must take your sign from the catcher with your back foot touching the front of the rubber, your hands apart, and your throwing hand at your side or in back of your body. Then get set with your hands together between your belt and chin, and hold that position for one second before delivering the ball to the plate.

You are not allowed to stop and start any movement toward the plate. If a left-hander's front leg goes across the imaginary line from first base to the pitcher's rubber during his knee lift, he must deliver the ball to the plate. If a left-hander's front leg goes more than 45 degrees toward home plate during his stride, he must deliver the ball to the plate. As a result of these limitations, base runners will watch a left-hander's front leg. Its position will reveal whether you are committing yourself to throw to the plate.

You do not need to throw over to first base a lot to limit base stealing. There are a number of techniques that a pitcher can use to discourage base stealing without having to make a pickoff throw at all. For starters, a quick delivery will cut back on the number of bases swiped while you're on the mound. Deliver the pitch to the plate in 1.3 seconds or less and your catcher will have an excellent chance of throwing out the runner. Here are some other methods.

1. Vary the length of time that you hold your set position—from the one-second minimum to three or four seconds, which will make it more difficult for the runner to get a start timed to the split second.

2. Hold your set position for three or four seconds, then step off. This tactic has the added benefit of allowing the hitter to potentially tip his hand, perhaps by sliding his hand down the bat for a bunt or squaring around in his stance. You can also fake a throw to first after stepping off, which you cannot do while your back foot is touching the rubber.

3. Quick-pitch. When you come to your set position and step off, most base runners retreat slowly to the base. Step back on the rubber, come to an accelerated set position, and deliver the pitch before the runner can reclaim his full lead. Be certain that you are set for a full second before throwing the pitch and that you don't overstride or rush your delivery.

4. Make a slide-step delivery. If you can maintain your timing with a slide step—minimizing the knee lift and moving right into a fall phase of throwing the ball—you can put a damper on base stealing.

Pickoff attempts come in many varieties. Some are based on trickery while others rely on quickness. Even your sequence of throws can nab a runner. For example, make a slow move to first base and then make a quick move. The accelerated move can sometimes take a runner by surprise and catch him before he gets back to the base.

Right-Handers' Move

Come to your set position with your feet shoulder-width apart or slightly closer, your right foot alongside the rubber, and your left foot a few inches forward of your right foot. Make sure you can see first base out of the corner of your eye. If you're not able to see the runner and the base easily, make an adjustment with your left foot. Angle it a few degrees toward first base from the imaginary line between the rubber and home plate.

Flex your knees slightly. Grip the ball inside the glove with your hands together between your sternum and the top of your uniform letters. Make the throw to first base by pivoting on the right foot and stepping toward the base. You can accelerate this move by simultaneously jumping and turning slightly off the ground and pivoting with both feet in the air. Make a short step with the left foot toward first base as you turn. Upon landing, you'll be in position to make a snap throw.

The throw should be short and quick, much like a catcher's pickoffs. Bring the ball quickly up and behind the ear and then throw it hard, aiming for a spot just below and to the left side of the first baseman's right knee.

Once a left-handed pitcher kicks his leg across the imaginary line between the pitching rubber and first base (toward second base), he must throw home. If he throws to first base, the umpire will call a balk.

When the right leg is lifted straight up, the pitcher has the option to throw to home plate or first base.

Left-Handers' Move

Left-handers have the distinct advantage of being able to throw to first base without turning. As you come to the set position, stare at the runner whether you intend to throw over or not. If the runner takes his eyes off you, throw over immediately.

When you reach the set position, shift your gaze to a point between first base and home plate that allows you to see both the batter and the

The pitcher displays a safe pickoff move to first base. His stride leg has unquestionably landed in the direction of first base.

This pickoff move is a greater risk and could attract a balk call. The stride leg has landed in a position that could be considered past the 45-degree mark between home plate and first base. The umpire may regard this move as being deceptive to the runner and award him second base.

base runner. You'll be able to see both without moving your head and the runner won't be able to read your eyes. Lift your knee so that it doesn't move across the imaginary line between the rubber and first base. Begin your fall toward home plate and make any throws to first before your foot lands beyond 45 degrees toward home plate. Aim your throw to the left and low side of the first baseman's right knee. Walking toward first base after you have delivered the throw can help "sell" the move to the umpire, that is, convince him that you did not deceive the runner by moving too far toward home plate before throwing to first base.

WHEN TO THROW OVER

Good times to try to pick off a runner:

- Two outs and the count is full
- One out, count full, man on first
- After a pitchout
- Base stealer on, breaking ball count (0–2, 1–2, 2–2)
- Hit-and-run counts (1–0, 2–1, 3–1)

24

CHANGING ARM SLOTS

"What makes him so successful is that you never know what to expect. He'll drop down sidearm and sneak a sidearm fastball on you, or a sidearm slider. You'll see him drop down and you're like, 'Oh no, what's coming now?' He has more different looks than anybody. And the stuff that comes from those different looks is as good as anyone's."
—DEAN PALMER (ON DAVID CONE)

Cy Young award winner David Cone is often referred to as the master of improvisation. He is notorious for throwing pitches from a variety of different arm angles to confuse and ultimately dispose of major league hitters. Because hitters are unable to anticipate Cone's release point, they're left guessing at what angle each pitch will leave his hand.

In addition, different arm angles have varying effects on the ball as it's released. Cone's slider breaks differently when thrown from a three-quarter delivery than when it's thrown sidearm. The same holds true for his fastball. If Cone throws an over-the-top fastball, a three-quarter delivery fastball, and a sidearm fastball, he's actually throwing three separate pitches because they each behave in a unique way. In essence, if a pitcher has three pitch types in his repertoire and throws each from three different angles, the batter actually has nine pitches to concern himself with.

Changing arm slots is a powerful tactic available to pitchers that is as productive as changing speeds and throwing to locations.

Soft Center/Hard Focus

It takes only four-tenths of a second for the ball to get from the pitcher's hand to the catcher's mitt. In that time, the batter has to pick up the ball,

143

identify its speed, pitch type, and location, decide whether or not to swing the bat, and finally, physically swing the bat. Hitters use what is called a soft center and hard focus. As the pitcher sets on the rubber and begins his delivery, the batter's eyes are in the mode of finding a soft center, which means his eyes are relaxed and gazing in a general area around the pitcher. It may be the pitcher's chest, head, or a sign on the center-field fence. The idea is to avoid a concentrated stare at an isolated target that causes the eyes to grow tired. The eyes can only stay focused for a limited amount of time. If the hitter strains to lock onto an area too early in the pitcher's delivery, the eyes lose their focus, or possibly even worse, blink. If either happens, the batter has relatively little chance of hitting the ball.

As the pitcher's arm rises up toward the point of release, the batter's eyes shift to a hard focus. He focuses sharply on the point of release so he can pick up the ball as soon as it leaves the pitcher's hand. The batter has a limited amount of time to decipher the pitch's type, speed, and location, so it's imperative that he track the ball immediately.

By changing arm slots, you'll upset the hitter's routine. He'll be unable to easily shift from soft center to hard focus because he'll be unable to predict where to shift his sights. As a result, the batter's eyes will become active earlier in the delivery. He'll attempt to follow the latter stages of your arm swing in his effort to anticipate the point of release. The batter's eyes will nervously dance around to find your slot, and possibly grow weary. With such heavy concentration on deciphering the point of release,

Changing arm slots from an over-the-top (left), three-quarter (center), or sidearm delivery (right) can disrupt the hitter's vision, timing, and ability to anticipate ball movement.

the batter's attention will be less than 100 percent focused on the actual pitch itself. Advantage—pitcher.

Changing arm slots also sends caution into the mind of the hitter. He'll lose a degree of aggressiveness and become somewhat defensive. Anytime you can introduce uncertainty into the mind-set of a batter, it works against him. His confidence sinks, as will his hitting prowess.

Varying Breaks and Movement

The advantage of changing arm slots is twofold. Not only will it disrupt the hitter's vision, but it also creates varying movements on your pitches. Fastballs and breaking balls respond differently when thrown from specific angles.

Fastball

In most cases, a fastball thrown over the top (released approximately near the one o'clock position) possesses the greatest velocity, but the least movement. Use a four-seam grip when throwing a fastball over the top. Because this pitch travels straight, throw it when you need a strike, when you're trying to pitch to or "paint" a corner of the plate, or if the hitter has trouble catching up to your fastball. If the hitter doesn't prove that he can handle the speed of your fastball, there is no reason to throw anything else.

Move your arm slot down to a three-quarter delivery (which rests halfway between over the top and sidearm) and the flight of your fastball will change. The ball (if you're a right-handed pitcher) will run in on right-handed hitters and tail away from left-handed hitters. Use your two-seam grip for this pitch and it will increase the movement on the ball. This pitch is best used to get in on the hands or "jam" same-side hitters, and coax opposite-side batters to hit the ball off the end of the bat. Most good hitters say that they'd rather hit a hard fastball that is straight than face a fastball of lesser velocity that moves.

A sidearm fastball is effective against same-side hitters. Do not throw this pitch to opposite-side hitters (right-hander versus left-hander or vice versa). They're able to pick the ball up easily and track it for a long time. Furthermore, sidearm fastballs travel on a flat plane with little or no downward movement. Flat pitches are more likely to be hit squarely and sent a long, long way.

Same-side hitters have trouble when a pitcher occasionally drops his arm angle down to throw sidearm. For starters, the ball appears as if it's heading straight for him. A common reaction by hitters is to step in the bucket; that is, they stride away from home plate. This tendency leaves the entire outside portion of the strike zone open for exploitation. Also, it's difficult to track this pitch. During the delivery, the pitcher's front shoulder tucks inward and hides the ball. It then flies open as the ball is released, creating a distraction. Before the hitter knows it, the ball is past him for a called strike.

Use a two-seam grip for a sidearm fastball. You can create a little run on the ball, and if you turn it over as you release it, the ball will sink.

Breaking Balls

Overhand breaking balls are commonly referred to as "12 to 6" breaking balls. This term originates from how the ball rotates in relation to the numbers on the clock. Straight downward rotation travels from 12 o'clock to 6 o'clock. Realistically, overhand breaking balls travel with a 1 o'clock to 7 o'clock (right-handed pitchers) or 11 o'clock to 5 o'clock (left-handed pitchers) rotation. This pitch breaks down and produces a lot of ground balls.

Throwing a breaking ball from a three-quarter delivery changes the rotation on the ball, and thus the direction of its break. Because more pressure is applied to the outside of the baseball as it's released, the rotation travels from 2 o'clock to 8 o'clock (right-handed pitchers) or 10 o'clock to 4 o'clock (left-handed pitchers). This pitch breaks sideways and downward. It will get you a lot of swings and misses, but if thrown in the wrong spot, can get battered. High-breaking balls or ones that cross through the middle of the strike zone can be sent soaring.

Much like the sidearm fastball, do not throw sidearm breaking balls to opposite-side hitters. It will break right into their wheelhouse. Sidearm benders are thrown to make same-side batters flinch or freeze as the ball breaks over the plate for a called strike. A second option is to throw the pitch so it breaks outside of the strike zone, hoping to lure the batter into chasing a bad pitch. Either way, this pitch should be thrown sparingly. If a same-side hitter sees this pitch a few times, he'll adjust and wait for that pitch to break into the strike zone. With its flat trajectory, this pitch can be hammered into tomorrow.

A Time and a Place

Changing arm slots can be very effective. Keep in mind, however, the importance of consistently throwing strikes. Most pitchers have a certain slot where they feel most comfortable throwing the ball accurately. Do not lose sight of this knowledge about yourself. Deception is a weapon, but not at the expense of sacrificing your ability to consistently throw strikes.

The best time to experiment and deceive is when you're ahead in the count. Use a different arm slot to surprise a hitter. With two strikes, drop down and give the hitter a look that's unfamiliar. Changing arm slots reaps the greatest benefits under these circumstances.

25

EXPANDING THE STRIKE ZONE

The artistry of Atlanta Braves pitchers Tom Glavine and Greg Maddux is remarkable to witness. Each possesses a fastball that has average or slightly above-average velocity by major league standards, yet their accomplishments are unmatched by any other pitching duo over the past decade. They've combined to win six Cy Young awards and carry winning percentages of .687 (Maddux) and .676 (Glavine) since 1991. Many factors, such as deceptiveness, changing speeds, experience, and wisdom have contributed to their achievements, but none more than their ability to locate pitches. In a day and age when radar guns register blazing fastballs that reach the mid to high 90s, Glavine and Maddux paint the corners of home plate and go about their business of getting batters out consistently.

Home plate measures 17 inches wide. The official baseball rules state that the ball must cross over that 17-inch plate to be called a strike. But because Maddux and Glavine are so accurate with their pitches, they're often able to expand the width of the strike zone beyond those 17 inches. By meticulously working the corners throughout the game, umpires can be lured into calling strikes on pitches that are just wide of home plate. Maddux and Glavine recognize this opportunity, and use the early stages of the game to seemingly brainwash umpires into calling a pitch a strike when it clearly misses to either side. Although hitters have become increasingly frustrated by their ability to expand the strike zone, the two wily veterans continue to stockpile wins and dominate major league lineups.

How to Expand the Strike Zone

The key to expanding the strike zone is accuracy. You've got to be able to throw the ball to specific locations with consistency. The quickest way to widen the strike zone is to throw to one corner of the plate over and over. Which corner should you throw to? Observe which side of the catcher the umpire stands over when calling balls and strikes. Most umpires stand to one side or the other, rarely standing directly behind the catcher. Throw to the side at which he is standing. Balls on that side of the plate will be centralized from his viewpoint. His strike zone will shift slightly toward the side where he's perched. Balls to the opposite side will appear farther away from him and out of the strike zone.

By continuously throwing pitches on the corner, the mind's eye of the umpire begins to consider these pitches to be the norm. They are perfect pitches. If the next pitch is a little off the plate (or less than perfect) the umpire's judgment tells him it's still a strike. He's been drawn in to thinking that the outside corner represents the middle portion of the plate, and

After the catcher gives the pitcher the sign for the type of pitch to be thrown (left), he shifts over to the outside part of the plate to give a target for location (right). Giving a centered target over the outside part of the plate can help to expand the strike zone.

something that is just off the plate now lies within the outside edge of the strike zone.

Glavine approaches hitters by pounding away at the outside corner and then occasionally throwing a pitch to the inside corner. Hitters have greater difficulty hitting the pitch on the outside corner. It's farther from their eyes, it entails letting the ball get deep in the strike zone before making contact (which is very hard to do), and because proper technique calls for minimal hip rotation, hitters produce less-powerful swings when hitting outside strikes. When Glavine expands the strike zone, batters are forced to swing at pitches outside of the strike zone. A ball outside is even more difficult to hit than an outside strike. It is especially tough to hit a ball outside with authority. Many batters simply attempt to foul the pitch off, and hope that Glavine's next pitch will offer something better to hit. Already, he's got them swinging in a defensive mode.

Glavine then throws a random pitch inside to keep the hitter honest, which stops the batter from leaning out over home plate in anticipation of an outside strike. If the hitter looks away and the pitcher throws a hard pitch inside, he has almost no chance of contacting the ball with the barrel of the bat.

Using Movement to Widen Home Plate

Another method of expanding the strike zone is throwing two-seam fastballs that tail or cut in and out of the strike zone. For example, say you're a left-handed pitcher facing a right-handed hitter. You've been successfully throwing four-seam fastballs to the outside part of the plate and are getting called strikes from the umpire. To make things even tougher on the hitter, grip the ball with the seams. Throw to the outside corner, but with a two-seam grip and slightly lower release point, the ball will tail away from home plate. The umpire, however, may recognize the early flight path of the pitch and anticipate the ball crossing over the plate. He'll raise his hand to call a strike, even though the ball moved away from the hitter as it entered the hitting zone and off the outside part of the plate.

You can also throw a two-seam fastball that starts inside off the plate, and then tails back over the inside corner. Maddux is notorious for baffling left-handed hitters with this pitch. Because the ball starts inside, batters immediately give up on the pitch. They decide not to swing. Before they realize the ball is going to tail back over the plate, it's too late to get the barrel on the ball. They can only swing the bat and get badly jammed, or take the pitch and hope the umpire calls it a ball.

Colorado left-hander Mike Hampton is a premier major league pitcher. He is extremely tough on hitters because he's able to make his fastball cut or tail. Not only are hitters faced with reacting to the location of Hampton's pitch, but also whether the ball will cut or tail during the late stages of its flight. Late movement freezes both hitters and umpires. Strike calls are often made if you're able to fool the umpire.

EXPANDING WITH TWO STRIKES

There is a second dimension to expanding the strike zone. If you get two strikes on the hitter and are ahead in the count (0–2, 1–2, 2–2), expand the strike zone horizontally or vertically in an attempt to get the hitter to chase something out of the strike zone.

Throughout the history of baseball, hitters have heard this cliché thousands upon thousands of times when they get two strikes: "Protect the plate." In other words, the hitter should swing at pitches on the perimeter of the strike zone, or ones that come close to that perimeter. With this in mind, throw pitches just outside the strike zone. Force them to swing the bat at a pitcher's pitch. Pitches just above or below the strike zone work just as well as pitches that are slightly inside or outside.

In addition, ask any umpire if he would rather call a ball or a strike. I guarantee the answer will be universal—strike. This feeling multiplies exponentially when there are two strikes in the count. The hitter better be swinging, or risk the sound of, "STTRRIIKKEE THREEEEE!!!!"

Assault and Battery

A good catcher is instrumental to expanding the strike zone. You make the pitch, but the catcher has to sell it with a believable presentation.

A catcher can help sell a pitch off the plate in two ways. The first lies in his setup. Instead of squatting directly behind home plate, he should shift his feet over to the side of the plate you're throwing to. His glove is still held in the center of his body, but it is now aligned with the edge of the plate, instead of the middle of home plate. Pitches thrown just off the plate are now received inside the catcher's shoulders, which looks much better than the catcher reaching out for the ball. When he reaches for the

Framing pitches that are slightly off the plate can give an umpire the impression that it crossed over the corner of the plate. The way a catcher receives and presents a pitch can make a big difference to the umpire calling balls and strikes.

ball, it sways the umpire's judgment—"the catcher reached for it, so it must be a ball."

The second way a catcher can help a pitcher is by framing the pitch. To frame a pitch, the catcher turns his glove inward toward home plate when receiving the pitch. A catcher can even frame pitches to expand the vertical strike zone. If the pitch is high, the catcher should move the glove downward as he receives the pitch. Low pitches should be raised upward upon receipt—show the white of the ball to the umpire and listen for "strike."

The strike zone is 17 inches wide. To get those pitches on the eighteenth and nineteenth inches called strikes, a skillful catcher is helpful.

26

DETECTING WEAKNESSES IN THE HITTER

"Everybody talks about Schilling's arm and great control, but nobody prepares for a start like he does. He studies the opposition's hitters like he's preparing for a test. He knows their strengths, weaknesses, the type of success they've had against him, and whether they're currently on a hot streak or slumping. He even knows who is going to be umpiring behind the plate and what his tendencies are."
—TERRY FRANCONA, FORMER PHILLIES MANAGER

There are more advantages to being a major league pitcher than you might imagine. Top-notch equipment, perfectly manicured ballparks, phenomenal defensive players, and a hefty paycheck are obvious perks, but the benefits run even deeper. By facing a lot of the same hitters game after game, month after month, and year after year, pitchers learn the strengths and weaknesses of hitters. They compile "the book" on hitters, which allows them to retire batters with the use of these scouting reports just as much as their change-ups and cut fastballs.

But what if you've never faced a hitter before? What if you've never even heard of the team before? At the amateur level—high school scheduled games, college road trips, and postseason tournaments—pitchers encounter lineups full of unfamiliar hitters. There is no way of addressing their tendencies, focusing on their weaknesses, or steering clear of their strengths. Is it simply your talent against mine and may the best man win? Well, not necessarily. Hitters tend to disclose their weaknesses and often put them on display for everyone to see. You've just got to know where to look.

Note: These statements you're about to read can be proven wrong from time to time. For example, it will be said that a player who has a hitch in his swing (drops his hands) will have difficulty handling high fastballs. In almost every case, that's true. That said, Barry Bonds has hit a lot of high fastballs that still haven't landed, and he has a hitch. So he is an exception to the rule. These recommendations are based on percentages, and baseball is a game of percentages. So if you notice a batter has a hitch and you attack him with a high fastball and he hits one so far it defies physics, our condolences. And if it's Bonds that hits it, well, if you're good enough to face the San Francisco Giants, you shouldn't need our advice anyway.

The Stance

A batting stance can tell you a lot of what you need to know about a hitter. Take what he shows you and use it to your advantage.

Commonly, hitters stand a certain way or in a certain spot to compensate for a weakness and promote particular strengths. For example, hitters who stand close to the plate like the ball inside, but have trouble handling pitches away. They move closer to the plate so the outside edge of the strike zone is now closer to them. Conversely, hitters who stand away from the plate do not like the ball inside, perhaps because of a long swing or slow hip rotation. Instead, they like the ball out away from them, so they move off the plate to push the inside strike outward.

Below is a list of general rules to follow. Take a moment on the mound to look for any of these tip-offs that expose a weakness.

Setup	Weakness
Wide stance	Fastballs up in the strike zone; breaking balls away
Narrow stance	Low strikes; off-speed pitches
Closed stance	Fastballs inside; low strikes
Open stance	Fastballs away; breaking balls away
Hands held high	Low strikes
Hands held low	High fastballs
Hands held away from the body	Fastballs inside and up
Hands held up close to head	Fastballs inside
Excessive movement	Off-speed pitches
No movement	Fastballs

An open stance (with a stride toward the hitter's pull side); pitch the batter away and feed him off-speed pitches or fastballs.

A closed stance (with a closed stride); pitch the batter inside with hard stuff.

Hands are held low; pitch the batter fastballs up in the strike zone.

Hands are held high; pitch the ball down in the strike zone.

Preswing Movements

Because you're concentrating on throwing pitches to specific target areas, it's difficult for you to recognize weaknesses in a batter's pre-swing movement. Some pitchers, such as Greg Maddux, can notice subtle movements during this stage that uncover useful information. But in most cases, you'll need the help of your catcher, teammates, and coaches.

A hitter's stride can be a major indicator of his strengths and weaknesses. If the batter strides closed (toward home plate), for example, he'll have difficulty hitting inside fastballs. His hips will be tied up and unable to fully rotate. As a result, the barrel of the bat will be late to the ball and he'll make contact below the sweet spot. Hard stuff inside will tie the hitter up all day.

Here are some other keys to look for in the pre-swing.

Preswing Movement	Weakness
Closed stride	Fastballs inside; low strikes
Open stride	Fastballs away; breaking balls away
Long stride	High fastballs; breaking balls away; off-speed pitches
Hitch (drop the hands)	High fastballs
Premature weight transfer	Off-speed pitches; fastballs inside; breaking pitches away
Wrapping the bat	Fastballs inside and up

The Swing

Measuring the swing and detecting its weaknesses is also a tough assignment while you're on the mound. Coaches and teammates can lend a helping hand. You don't necessarily have to pick out the mechanical flaw in the swing, though. Focus on the results. The way the ball is struck can be telling.

Every pitcher notices when a hitter can't catch up to his fastball. In this case, continue to pump the heat. Don't throw something off-speed and speed up your opponent's bat. Challenge him with fastballs on the inside part of the plate until he proves that he can handle it.

Pulled foul balls indicate two factors to consider. The hitter's swing is early and he's looking for pitches middle-in. Counter by mixing in an off-speed pitch or locating pitches on the outside part of the plate. An off-speed pitch thrown to the outside corner can really give the hitter fits.

Batters hitting pop-fly foul balls are catching the bottom of the ball. The barrel of the bat may be dipping as it enters the hitting zone (an uppercut). Try to coax the hitter into climbing the ladder. Throw fastballs up in the strike zone and see if you induce a pop-up or swing and miss.

> *"Hitters take pitches certain ways, they foul off pitches certain ways. You try to anticipate what they're looking for as best you can. But you never know for sure. Anticipate the best you can and pitch accordingly."*
>
> —GREG MADDUX

Chopped ground balls indicate the opposite. The batter is catching the top of the ball. Perhaps he's rolling his top hand over prematurely. Locate pitches down in the strike zone and try to get a ground ball.

Detecting a hitter's weakness makes your job easier. Hopefully, you'll be able to utilize the information to your advantage and record outs at a faster rate throwing fewer pitches. Remember, your goal is to record outs, not strikeouts.

A hitter who uses an open stance or strides open will pull off the ball. With his hips and shoulders flying open, he'll be left only with his arms to hit off-speed and outside strikes. Exploiting a hitter's weakness can earn you some quick and easy outs.

BASERUNNING

In this next section, you'll read about plays that focus specifically on baserunning. Many might ask, how can a baserunning situation be considered a game-breaking play? If you're one of those inquirers, you might want to pose that question to the Oakland Athletics.

During the 2001 wild card playoff series, the A's held a two games to none lead over the New York Yankees. Returning to their home stadium, Oakland needed just one victory to close out the Yanks in the five-game series.

Holding a 1–0 lead in the seventh inning, Mike Mussina yielded a base hit to Jeremy Giambi. Terrence Long then came to the plate and laced a two-out double down the right-field line. Giambi, not the swiftest of runners, had no thought but to score the tying run.

Yankee right fielder Shane Spencer uncorked a throw that sailed over the head of first base cutoff Tino Martinez. Giambi never broke stride, but by seeing the overthrow, he may have thought there would be no play at the plate.

Shortstop Derek Jeter, who noticed the throw was high out of Spencer's hand, darted across the infield to field the ball on one bounce. He then backhand-flipped the ball to catcher Jorge Posada.

Giambi attempted to cross home plate standing up. Again, he may not have thought there was a potential play at the plate with Spencer missing the cutoff. Posada received Jeter's flip in front of home plate, dove back to his left, and grazed Giambi's calf before he touched home plate. The umpire called Giambi out, the inning was over, and the A's ended up losing the game 1–0. They went on to lose the next two games, as the Yankees advanced to the American League Championship Series.

Had Giambi slid to the right side of home plate, Posada would have had no chance of tagging him in time to record the out. Giambi would have scored a run and tied the game, which could have altered the results of the game and series. Giambi's baserunning error was crucial, and changed the momentum of the series in favor of New York. He committed a cardinal baserunning sin, which is that if there is a close tag play on the base paths, you must slide.

Instinct, Awareness, and Efficiency

Baserunning is a fundamental skill that requires instinct, awareness, and efficiency. Any player on a roster can be a good base runner. Speed is an asset, but it does not ensure competence. Fast runners who take uneducated risks or fail to exploit defensive breakdowns and weaknesses are more detrimental to a team than runners who are slow-footed.

Instinct is acquired through experience. Play in as many games as possible to become familiar with the nuances of the game. Through time, you'll develop the ability to know when a flare to the outfield will drop safely, how deep an outfielder needs to field the ball for you to advance an extra base, and how to identify breaking pitches that will bounce in the dirt, which allows you to break for the next base while the ball is still in flight.

Awareness means understanding the game situation—what inning it is, what the score is, how many outs there are, and who is up at the plate. It also means knowing the strengths, weaknesses, and tendencies of the opposing defense. Where is the left fielder playing? How strong is the catcher's arm? What pitch does the pitcher throw when he's ahead in the count? Which direction is the wind blowing? All of these factors, and many more, influence the game and contribute to your decision of whether to take an educated risk or yield on the bases.

To develop efficient baserunning skills takes practice. Work on making good turns, minimize your angles when rounding a base, practice your jumps to eliminate unnecessary steps or movements. Proper running technique can reduce the number of steps it takes you to get from one base to the next. One more or one less step can mean the difference between being called safe or out.

If you think baserunning can't make or break a team's quest for victory, you're sorely mistaken. The following section deals with several baserunning plays that are just as important to master as hitting a 1–2 breaking ball or turning a 3-6-3 double play.

27

ADJUSTING YOUR SLIDE TO THE PLAY AT THE BASE

In Game 7 of the 1992 National League Championship series, the Atlanta Braves trailed the Pittsburgh Pirates 2–1 with two outs in the ninth inning. With the bases loaded, unheralded third-string catcher Francisco Cabrera stood at home plate. With only 10 at-bats during the entire regular season, Cabrera was virtually unknown and seemed unworthy of holding the fate of Atlanta's quest to return to the World Series.

David Justice represented the tying run on third base, while veteran first baseman Sid Bream stood on second base. Bream was never a swift runner, and several knee operations throughout his career further diminished his running speed.

With two strikes, Cabrera achieved the unthinkable. He laced Stan Belinda's pitch to left field for a base hit. Justice scored easily to tie the game and Bream chugged around third base, desperately racing to reach home base safely and clinch the team's return to the Fall Classic. The throw from left fielder Barry Bonds was slightly off-line. Pirate catcher Mike LaValliere stepped to his right to field the throw from Bonds. Bream slid to the foul territory side of home plate as LaValliere dove back to apply the tag. Bream's left foot swiped across home plate an instant before leather grazed his leg. The umpire called Bream "Safe!" and 51,975 Atlanta fans broke into a jubilant celebration.

Cabrera was the unlikely hero, but the slide by Bream certainly deserves its due attention. What Bream lacked in speed, he made up for with savvy baserunning. He noticed the catcher moved toward the infield side of home plate to receive the ball and correctly slid to the opposite slide. Instinctive plays such as that one are what win ballgames, or in this case, a National League pennant.

Different Slides for Different Situations

It's understood that when you're involved in a close play on the base paths, you've got to slide. How you slide depends on the circumstances. There are five basic slides we'll discuss: the bent-leg slide, pop-up slide, hook slide, fake hook slide, and head-first slide.

Bent-Leg Slide

This basic slide is used when there is a close play at the base. The defensive player receiving the ball is set in position to make the catch and apply the tag. You are running to the base at top speed, determined to beat the throw.

About 10 to 12 feet from the base, begin to break into your slide. Take your final step with your left foot, and lean back and throw your arms up in the air. Leap forward off your left foot and land on your lower back and rear end. As you extend forward, bend your left leg inward so your left foot folds under your right knee. Extend your right leg and foot out to the base.

It's important to throw the hands up as you begin your slide. Injuries to the hands, and especially the thumbs, are suffered when base runners attempt to brace their fall with their hands. Keep them up and out of harm's way.

The bent-leg slide. Keep the arms and hands raised to avoid injury.

Be smart when deciding which region of the base to target with your slide and lead foot. Say, for example, you're stealing second base. Because the throw is coming from the catcher and closer to the front of the base, slide for the back of the base. If the infielder receives the ball in front of the base, he'll have to reach back to tag you out. Conversely, if you're sliding into second base and the throw is coming from right field, aim for the front of second base. The receiver sets up to catch the ball on the outfield side of the base.

Pop-up Slide

Pop-up slides are used on errant throws. They allow you to quickly get back up on your feet and advance to the next base. As you approach the base, glance to see if the fielder is getting ready to pick up or block a throw in the dirt, or if he's preparing to jump for a high throw. In either situation, a pop-up slide is warranted.

Break into your slide a step later than you would for a bent-leg slide. Don't lean all the way back, but rather sit nearly upright as your rear end slides across the ground. Extend to the base with your right foot, and use

If there is no throw or the ball gets past the fielder, use the pop-up slide to be in position to advance to the next base.

the base to pop yourself up. Push off the ground with your left foot and rise up on both feet. If the ball gets past the infielder, continue running to the next base.

This slide is generally used when you know you have beaten the throw to the base. Watch how the fielder is reacting and take advantage of an errant throw. Always maintain an aggressive attitude on the base paths.

Hook Slide

There are two types of hook slides that you can learn and use in game situations. The first is the traditional hook slide and the second is the fake hook slide. Both are used when the throw beats you to the base and you need to slide to a safer area in hopes of avoiding the tag.

Imagine you're standing on first base, and your teammate hits a single to right field. You start going like gangbusters to advance all the way to third base. When you're about halfway between second and third base, you realize there is going to be a play. Your third base coach is pointing to the ground, indicating that you're going to have to slide. As you take your final approach steps, you see the third baseman track the ball and then catch it with his backhand. You're about to break your slide and he's already caught the ball. A hook slide is definitely in order.

Stay to the left-field side of third base. Start your slide just before you reach the base. Instead of sliding directly into the bag, slide approximately

If you notice the fielder is set up to receive the ball on a particular side of the base, use the hook slide. A fake hook slide is preferable when the ball beats you to the base and you need to avoid the tag.

two feet to the right of the base. Bend your left leg outward, rather than inward. Your right leg extends past the base, and as the rest of you skids past the bag, your left foot reaches out and hooks onto the back of third base.

The purpose of using this slide is that the third baseman will instinctively extend to apply his tag to the front of the base. If your foot, leg, or body is not there to tag or within his reach, you can't be tagged out. By the time he's able to readjust his tag, you'll have already slid past the base and hitched safely with your left foot.

Fake Hook Slide

Use the fake hook slide if the ball beats you handily. The side of the base where the ball is fielded dictates the side of the base where you'll execute the slide. For example, say you line a base hit to center field and try to stretch it into a double. The throw is coming from center field, so slide to the left of second base, extend with the left leg, and bend your right knee inward.

Slide far enough to the left of the base so the infielder will be unable to reach you. After you pass the base, swing your left arm over and reach for the back of the bag. As you do this, you'll flop over onto your stomach. You're hoping to fake out the infielder and catch him out of position and unable to apply the tag in time.

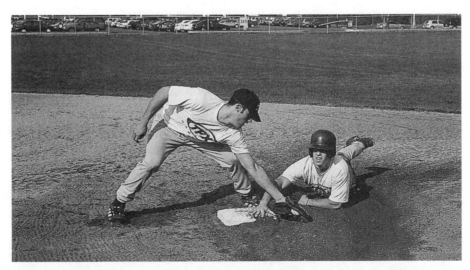

Slide past the base to the opposite side from that the fielder occupies. Turn over toward the base and reach out with your hand to grab the back of the bag.

Head-First Slide

Any player with lightning-fast wheels aspires to be the next Rickey Henderson or Kenny Lofton. Images of those gifted runners evoke visions of head-first slides. It is the fastest way to slide into a base, but is also the most dangerous.

Head-first slides are quicker because of your approach. Instead of decelerating and leaning back to slide in feetfirst, you're able to continue accelerating forward with your legs. You simply bend slightly more at the waist from the running position and dive forward. A faster approach gets you to your point of destination in less time.

As you leave your feet to dive forward, push your arms outward until they're nearly extended. Land on your wrists and forearms first to brace your fall. Your arms must land flat and firm to maintain your forward momentum. Your midsection then hits the ground followed by your thighs and feet.

Keep your fingers pointed up and out as they approach the base. Your goal is to reach the base with the pads of your fingers. As you reach the base, grab the top of the base with your fingers and turn your head away from the throw to protect your face. Hold onto the base with one hand, and request a time-out from the umpire with your opposite.

Injuries occur frequently during head-first slides, which is why they are not used 100 percent of the time. Players sprain wrists when they land, jam fingers reaching for the base, and injure their shoulders if they slide into the base too late. Do not use this method of sliding unless you're able to execute it safely, and are aware of the risks involved.

If executed correctly, the head-first slide is the fastest method of reaching the base.

28

STEALING THIRD BASE

Baseball tacticians often preach that third base is easier to steal than second base. If that's true, why do we see so many base runners stealing second base, and so few stealing third? Well, there are plenty of answers to that, but before delving into that discussion, let's focus on the subject at hand.

The biggest difference between stealing third base and second base is that you almost always steal third base on the pitcher, not on the catcher. More often than not you steal second base on a pitcher who has a slow delivery to the plate. However, a catcher who has slow feet, long arm action, or a weak delivery also can help you steal second.

The throw from catcher to third base is very short—only 90 feet compared to the 120-foot throw to second base. So the theft has to be committed by taking advantage of the pitcher. There are several ways to accomplish this goal: a big lead, the pitcher fails to make you stop, predictable patterns in his delivery, a lack of attention. Any one of these factors can unlock the vault and swing the door open to an uninvited visit to the hot corner.

A Big Lead

Unlike first base, no one is standing on second base to hold you on, which allows you more freedom to roam. The shortstop and second baseman have the responsibility of holding you close, but they're also concerned about their territory. The more they cheat over toward second base, the less ground they can cover.

Keep increasing the distance of your lead to see how much you can get. If you can stretch it to 15 or 20 feet, you've only got 70 or 75 feet to go.

A big lead coupled with a good jump will make it nearly impossible for the catcher to throw you out. Use your first and third base coaches as your eyes. If a middle infielder breaks to the base behind you, your base coaches are there to alert you to retreat immediately.

Make sure your lead is even with the base if you're considering stealing. The shortest distance between two points is a straight line. Don't take steps back toward deep shortstop and break from that position. You're increasing your distance to third base. Break from a point directly between second and third base.

Walking Lead

Pitchers will admit that once the runner is off first base, they pay less attention to him and focus on the batter. Take advantage of this trend. Casually walk off of second base, and continue walking toward third base. This stroll not only increases your lead, but also keeps you moving forward. Breaking for third base from a walking lead puts you at full speed much faster than breaking from a stationary lead. Would you rather start a race from a dead standstill, or already in motion?

Keep your feet moving as you take your lead off second base. This tactic not only increases your lead, but also keeps the body in motion, which improves your jump. If the pitcher doesn't stop you, take all that you can get.

To pull off the walking lead, stay relaxed. Don't creep too far off the base immediately or expose a look of guilt. Stroll off the base as if you're not up to anything. In other words, appear as if you're not about to steal. Don't do anything to alarm the pitcher. Stay cool and casual to maintain the element of surprise.

Predictable Pattern of Delivery

Pitchers get into patterns, much like batters have pre-stance routines. (Just be thankful that Nomar Garciaparra is not a pitcher.) Take note of whether the pitcher has a predictable pattern of delivery. Does he look at you, look back home, and then lift his leg? Does he look back at you twice, then throw home? If he displays a distinct pattern, take advantage. If he looks at you, looks home, and then throws, take off when he turns his head to home plate. The catcher will have no chance of throwing you out.

Part of stealing third base is taking educated risks. Anticipation and selective aggressiveness are critical. Take what the pitcher gives you, and you'll take third base.

Why Stealing Third Is Not as Popular as Stealing Second

Let's clarify one implicit rule when running the bases: do not attempt to steal third base with two outs. It's senseless and can take the bat out of a hitter's hands with a runner in scoring position. If you're thrown out, the inning is over. If you slide in safely, you still need a hit to score you, so there is no point of taking the risk. Only if the pitcher forgets that you're on base and starts his delivery from the windup is it okay to steal third base because there is no risk involved.

If you follow this rule, it already eliminates 33 percent of the time you can steal third base. That percentage only partially explains why runners attempt to steal second more often than third base.

Coaches command players to steal second base to move them into scoring position. From first base, it takes two hits to plate the runner. From second base, it takes just one hit to score the run. A runner on second base presents a threat to the defense, and a great opportunity for the offense.

Usually, the sign to steal second base is flashed to give the batter an opportunity to drive in a run. It's then left up to the hitter to produce.

Stealing third base with less than two outs, however, can increase your team's chances of scoring a run. A fly ball to the outfield scores you from third base. With the infield playing back, a ground ball to the infield scores you from third base. A wild pitch, passed ball, base hit, suicide squeeze, or errant throw from the catcher scores you from third base. Staying at second base leaves you in scoring position, but you're a greater threat to score by occupying third base.

The crossover step is critical when stealing third base. Turn your body so your shoulders are square to third base and push off with your right foot. Quickness, the ability to get to top speed in a short period of time, is the key to stealing third base.

STEALING ONE OFF THE DEFENSE

Runners on first and second base with nobody out in the late innings of a close game usually calls for a sacrifice bunt. The runner from second advances to third base and can now score in any number of ways. The runner from first advances into scoring position.

The defense may call for one of several bunt coverages. One is the rotation play, which has the third baseman charging and the shortstop moving over to cover third base. Another bunt coverage has the third baseman stay at the base, while the pitcher is responsible for fielding balls to his right. At times, a defense can get caught in a defensive lapse in a regular rotation. The third baseman charges too far too soon, the shortstop covers the force at second base, the second baseman moves to first base, and the first baseman charges. The third baseman has left his base open.

If you are on second base and see that third is open, take off. Hopefully, the batter will recognize that you have the base stolen and pull the bat back. Now you're standing on third base, and the hitter has an opportunity to swing the bat without sacrificing an out.

29

GETTING A GOOD LEAD AND JUMP ON BATTED BALLS

Highlight shows cast by television networks focus on performance acts that dazzle audiences. The prodigious home run, the blazing fastball, the astounding field play are showcased as the game-breaking moments that dictate the outcome of a baseball game. Rarely do you see the sacrifice bunt that set up the game-winning hit, the great change-up thrown

Take a moment to check the positioning of the outfielders before taking your lead. Repeat this check on every pitch.

that is weakly popped up to help escape a jam, or the outfield defensive positioning taken before a pitch that allowed the outfielder to make a running catch at the warning track. These significant contributions to victories are victims of television editing and perish on the cutting-room floors of television studios. They are not given their just due in the eyes of the casual fan.

Baseball players and aficionados alike know better. It's the little things that help build a lead or stave off an offensive attack. Getting a good lead and jump on a batted ball is a prime example of a hidden skill that can pay huge dividends to a ball club.

Getting a Good Lead

To take a good lead, review the proper method of getting off the base. Address the sign from your third base coach and then pick up the pitcher to make sure it's safe to leave the base. Flex your knees and bend at the waist.

From first base, your first step is the opposite of a crossover step. Instead of crossing your left leg in front of the your right, step behind your right foot with the left foot to protect yourself from a quick pickoff attempt. If you cross over your right foot, your feet can get tangled up as you try

When taking the first step of your lead, step behind your right leg with your left foot (as shown). Crossing your left foot in front of your right leg puts you in a vulnerable position if the pitcher quickly throws to first base.

Keep your eyes on the pitcher at all times as you take your lead. Continue to increase your lead by taking short steps with your right, and then left foot. Also, make sure your lead is in a direct line with second base.

to get back to first. Slide your left foot behind your right to avoid tripping yourself up.

After your initial step, take two or three slide steps. The right foot extends out toward second base, and the left foot then slides over to meet up with the right foot. Keep your eyes on the pitcher at all times. Move to an area that represents the farthest possible point from first base that you can still get back to the base safely on a pickoff throw. If the pitcher throws over and you get back easily, add another step to your lead. If he throws again and you're still confident about getting back, add another half-step to your lead.

THE BENEFITS OF AN AGGRESSIVE LEAD

A big lead is advantageous for obvious reasons. A steal of second base becomes a little easier because you're reducing the distance between first and second base. It also gives you a better chance of beating a force play to second base on a ground ball, and advancing to third base or home plate on a hit.

Aggressive leads also have an adverse effect on the pitcher. He'll notice the size of your lead and become concerned. He may throw over several times or speed up his delivery to the plate. Either way, his attention has lost a degree of focus on his immediate enemy—the hitter. If the pitcher is worried about what the base runner is doing, he's more likely to make a mistake with a pitch to the batter. Hanging breaking balls or catching too much of home plate with fast-balls are common mistakes that lead to extra-base hits.

By taking an aggressive lead you're not just helping your chances of advancing, but you're also helping the hitter's odds of getting a good pitch. Create a diversion for your teammates and draw some attention with a big lead.

After the pitch is thrown, take a few shuffle steps toward second base to slice into the distance to second base and build some momentum. Time your shuffle so that your right foot is planted on the ground as the pitch crosses home plate. If the ball is taken for a ball or swung at and missed, push off your right foot and cross it over your left en route back to the base. The catcher may snap a throw down to the first baseman.

Take larger leads from second and third base. No player is standing on the bag holding you on, and pickoff attempts from the pitcher are rare. Keep moving forward until the pitcher turns to you, forcing you to stop. From a stationary position, continue to increase your lead with small slide steps. If the pitcher doesn't stop you, keep moving and build momentum.

Understand the situation as you take your lead from second and third base. If you're looking to steal third base, position yourself even with the bases. Under all other circumstances, take a few steps back toward the outfield. You will create an angle to third base that will allow you to reach the base and continue running at full speed without making a big turn.

From third base, always take your lead in foul territory. A batter might hit a hard line drive or ground ball down the third-base line. If the ball hits you in fair territory, you're out. Stay in foul territory to avoid killing a rally with a bonehead play.

Getting a Good Jump

Note: For the purpose of this entry, we'll assume that each running situation calls for the runner to advance to the next base. A runner on second base or third base, runners on second and third, or runners on first and third do not apply. The runner must advance if the ball is hit on the ground.

On balls hit to right and right-center field, pick up your third base coach as you approach second base. Because you can't see the play, use the eyes of your third base coach and follow his direction.

The best base runners have great instincts. They know when the ball leaves the bat whether it will be caught or fall safely for a hit. Instinct is developed out on the baseball field. It cannot be learned in a classroom or conditioned in a weight room. You've got to play a lot of baseball games, and pay attention when you're doing so.

Check to see where the defense is playing. Are the outfielders shallow, deep, or at regular depth? Are they shaded toward right or left field, or playing straight away? What kind of arms do they have? You should have absorbed this information during pregame infield/outfield practice.

The first item of concern at contact is the trajectory of the ball off of the bat. If the ball is hit on the ground, immediately sprint to the next base. As you're running, look to see if the ball escapes through the infield. If so, quickly break into a turn and look to advance to the next base. Use your third base coach if you're running from first base. Balls hit to right-center and right field are out of your field of vision. Pick up the third base coach and see if he is waving you on to advance or telling you to stop and hold second base.

If the ball is hit in the air, make an educated guess as to whether the ball will drop safely or be caught. Again, checking first to see where the outfielders are positioned is critical on questionable balls hit in the air.

If you're sure the ball will drop, don't hesitate. Run hard and get as many bases as you can. You'll rarely be criticized for being aggressive on the base paths. On questionable balls that are hit shallow, advance halfway between the base you're holding and the next base. If it's caught, you're able to get back. If it drops, you can advance. Don't stay on your base and watch because you can be thrown out on a force play.

On questionable balls hit deep, consider the base you're standing on. If you're on first base, run all the way to second base. If the ball drops, you should be able to score. If it's caught, you'll have plenty of time to get back to first.

From second base, it depends on the number of outs. If there are no outs, stay near the base so you can tag up. If the ball drops, you'll still be able to score. If it's caught, you can tag up and advance to third. You're now standing on third base with less than two outs. With one out, move halfway between second and third base, which makes scoring certain if the ball drops. If it's caught, retreat back to second base. You're still in scoring position with two outs. With two outs, run on contact.

From third base, always go back to the base on balls hit in the air. If it drops, you can practically walk home. If it's caught, listen to your third base coach for whether you should tag up.

Aggressive leads, instinctive jumps, and intelligent decision making represent the nuts and bolts of a good base runner. Speed is great, but it's only an asset. Average runners can be great base runners, and fast runners can be terrible. Take the time to make baserunning a strength in your game.

30

BREAKING UP A DOUBLE PLAY

It's often called a "twin killing." Just when the offense thinks it has something going, the defense fields a hard-hit ball, flips to a base for a force-out, and then fires to first to complete the double play. With one swing of the bat, two outs are recorded, squandering chances of a big inning. The wind drops out of your sails on offense, and the game's momentum quickly shifts to your opponent.

As a runner on base, it's your responsibility to do what it takes to make sure that double play is not turned. That means sprinting as soon as you recognize the ball is on the ground, sliding hard into the base, and breaking up the double play. Force an errant throw, cause the fielder to double-clutch before throwing, become entangled in his legs so he's unable to release his throw. Do whatever you need to do to disrupt the throw of the middle infielder attempting to turn two.

What the Rules Permit

Breaking up double plays is as much a part of the game as bunts, wild pitches, or ground-rule doubles. The intent is to slide into the feet of the fielder attempting to make the throw to first base. That way, he'll be unable to stride and make a strong throw or he'll have to take to the air to throw the ball. Your intent is not to injure or hurt the player, but to disrupt the completion of the double play.

Most infielders are taught not to stand on or in front of the base—in other words, to stay out of harm's way. They position themselves to one side of the base or behind it for protection from the runner, so you have to counter their defense.

The rule states that you're allowed to slide in the area of second base as long as a hand can reach the base. If your hand cannot reach the base the umpire will call you out for offensive interference. Offensive interference is an act by the team at bat that interferes with, obstructs, impedes, hinders, or confuses any fielder attempting to make a play. The umpire may also call out the batter-runner attempting to reach first base if he judges that the play would have been made successfully if the interference had not occurred.

As you're running to the base, observe how the infielder is setting up to take the throw. Determine the location from which he'll throw the ball and direct your slide to that area. Get as close as you can to the fielder and break into your slide just before the infielder receives the ball. Delaying the slide allows you to maintain your speed and prolong the sound of your "footsteps" as long as possible. Footsteps are what the fielder hears as he awaits the throw. They act as a psychological distraction.

Using a bent-leg slide, extend your lead foot directly into the feet of the thrower. Point your toe and keep your cleats down. Slide with the intention of traveling into and through the legs of your opponent—aggressively. However, do not rise up as in a football-like blocking move.

Automatic Double Plays

Follow the rules or you'll create an automatic double play. By not sliding in the general vicinity of the base, by intending to hurt the opposing player, or by not sliding at all, you will be called out, as will the runner at first base. Sliding too far away from the base is against the rules. It's the same as if you were to run out of the baseline. But by unfairly obstructing the fielder's attempt to throw to first base, the batter is also called out.

Attempting to hurt a player is simply not tolerated in baseball. It's a breach of etiquette and could be grounds for an ejection. Sliding with your spikes up or diving into the player are not permitted and will result in two outs.

Failing to slide is also cause for the umpire to call both runners out. First, there is no excuse for not sliding. Whether it's because you're not hustling or trying to prevent the throw from the infielder, it's not acceptable in a baseball game. Get your pants dirty—slide.

On double-play balls, your job as the base runner is to do whatever it takes (within the rules) to stop that throw from getting to first base in time to complete the double play. Your hustle can keep an inning alive, giving your teammates an opportunity to produce more runs.

Turns from Third and Home Plate

Double-play turns are not limited to second base. Double plays can be made from third base and home plate as well. Regardless of the base, it's still your job to break up the double play if the first throw of a double play comes to the bag you're approaching.

A fairly common play is the bases-loaded come-backer to the pitcher. The pitcher's job is to throw the ball directly to the catcher, who will then throw to first base. As the runner on third base, bust your tail down the line and get to the catcher before he's able to make a throw. Slide into his feet at home plate to prevent the double play.

A common mistake players make is that they become lethargic and slow their run to home. By hustling all the way to the plate and breaking up the throw, you can keep the inning alive and the bases will remain loaded for the next hitter.

Breaking up double plays requires two things. It requires hustle and a sense of teamwork. You'll be forced out, but by running aggressively, you can help your teammate reach base safely.

INDEX